Learn Mexican for Adult Beginners Workbook

Speak Mexican Spanish in 30 Days!

Table of Contents

Complete Spanish Phrasebook

+ Digital Spanish Flashcards Download

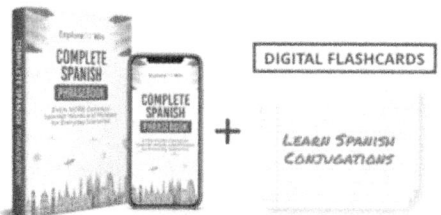

Scan QR code above to claim your free bonuses

OR

visit exploretowin.com/vipbonus

Ready To Start Speaking Spanish?

✓ **Say what you want:** learn the most common words and phrases used in Spanish, so you can express yourself clearly, the first time!

✓ **Avoid awkward fumbling:** explore core Spanish grammar principles to avoid situations where you're left blank, not knowing what to say.

✓ **Improved recall:** Confidently express yourself in Spanish by learning high-frequency verbs & conjugations - taught through fun flashcards!

Scan QR code above to claim your free bonuses

OR

visit exploretowin.com/vipbonus

Introduction

¡Bienvenido! How are you? So, we've heard you want to learn Spanish. But not any kind of Spanish; you want to learn Mexican Spanish, one of the most popular, creative and musical variations there are. You want to learn the language of Frida Kahlo, Octavio Paz, Pancho Villa, and Salma Hayek; the language of Guillermo del Toro and Carlos Santana. The language of the most populous Spanish-speaking country in the world: Mexico!

There are plenty of good reasons for anyone to want to study Mexican Spanish. You may be planning a trip, a short vacation or a long road trip. Or you may be curious about this variety of Spanish. You may have your own secret or private reasons (we won't ask, don't worry). Anyway, no matter the purpose, you're in luck! You've come to the right place.

In this book, you'll find a quick introductory course on Mexican Spanish. Our aim is that when you reach the end of the book, you'll be able to start and maintain a basic conversation on the most common topics, such as food, work, shopping, and many more! It's not an easy task, but don't worry, with patience and perseverance, you're going to make it. If almost 600 million people all over the world can speak Spanish—of which 130 million speak Mexican Spanish—there is no reason to believe you can't speak it too.

As you know, Rome wasn't built in a day, so, if we want this to work, we have to take it step by step. Languages are idiosyncratic and capricious, and Spanish is no exception. In many ways, it works similar to English; in many others, it doesn't. That's why, we're going to start with the basics: how to strike up a conversation, how to ask questions, and the differences between Mexican and European Spanish. We'll read about some grammar too, but only a little bit—the present tense, mostly, and a small pesky rule called *concordancia* ("agreement").

After that, we're going to learn about the past tense, we are going to have some fun with Mexican idioms, and we're going to revisit some of the most usual topics and conversational situations. You want to be able to speak in Spanish both in an airport and in a restaurant, don't you? Well, we're going to make sure you can do that—and much more.

The final part of the book will focus on other aspects of Mexican culture, like music and festivities. Of course, there will be some grammar too, mainly the future tense. But don't be scared; we use grammar mostly as a foothold, a tool to clarify some otherwise confusing aspects. After all, we don't want you to be a Spanish scholar. We just want you to speak your mind! We want, as a famous Spanish idiom says, for you to be able to *hablar hasta por los codos* (literally, "talk even through the elbows").

However, you know how this is: you can't learn anything without practice. So this is not only a textbook—it's a workbook. After each chapter, you'll find a series of exercises for you to practice what you've learned. The answers will be on the following page—but try to solve the exercises on your own, without peeking. Once you are done, you can check the answers. Bear in mind that mistakes are a necessary step in every learning process, so, hopefully, you're going to make some. That's okay, it's important to have faith in the process.

If you read the explanations carefully and complete the exercises, by the time you finish this book, you'll be able to maintain a basic conversation in Spanish. You'll know, of course, how to say hello, goodbye, sorry and please—the most basic kind of human interaction. But you'll also be able to ask for directions, order food, bargain—don't do it too much—and make small talk with almost anyone. You'll also be used to the intricacies of Mexican Spanish, that small wrinkles that make it different from all other Spanish varieties around the world.

You may wonder how we are so sure about it. Where do we get our confidence? How do we know that you'll be able to achieve all that? Well, let's say that we've learned—like everyone else, like you will—from our experience. This book is part of a long-lasting project. In the last few years, we've pointed our efforts towards one main goal: make people fluent *fast*. Languages are a tool, a link that connects people all over the world, and we want you, and everyone else, to master it in the easiest way possible.

How we plan to do that, you may be asking yourself. Well, that's no secret; in fact, it's in the book! You just have to keep reading. We're not going to entertain you with this introduction any longer. Just turn the page and plunge into the fascinating world of Mexican Spanish. *¡Hasta luego!*

Chapter 1: *¡Hola!* How to Start a Conversation

Hablar no es diferente de pensar: hablar es pensar.

- Octavio Paz

Every good story starts with a conversation. It's the oldest trick in the book: two people that don't know each other have a little chat in a bar, a ship, or a train. Whether you end up like *Titanic, Before Sunrise* or *Strangers On a Train*—three good movies, but with very different endings—is entirely up to you.

However, starting a conversation can be tricky, especially if you are not doing it in your first language. At the beginning, besides greetings, we usually find a lot of conventions and courtesy formulas, which can be very difficult to decipher. Moreover, these conventions tend to be different in different Spanish-speaking countries: Mexicans and Uruguayans don't necessarily open a conversation in the same way.

That first exchange is also when the tone of the conversation— formal or informal—is settled. And it's usually the time when we are most worried about being kind: you'll find a lot of pleases, thank yous and your welcomes on these stages. You don't necessarily have to become rude after gaining confidence, of course, but you know what I mean. First impressions are important.

So this is what we're going to do in this first chapter of the book: we're going to work on how to start a conversation. This means we're going to deal with:

- Greetings: *hola* ("hello"), *adios* ("goodbye"), and everything in between
- Polite words, like *por favor* ("please") and *perdón* ("sorry")
- Present tense, the easiest of all
- Formal and informal treatment
- Difference between *tú* (informal "you") and *usted* (formal "you")
- Basic personal introductions

Hola y adiós

In English there are several ways of saying "hello". We have, for example, "hello", "hi", or "good morning". Each of these terms has a slightly different vibe. Some are more formal than others, and some can only be used at certain times of the day. Well, the same can be said of Spanish.

The most standard greeting is *hola*. It can be translated as "hello". It's very easy to use, as it's mostly an all rounder. Here you can see a few examples:

- *¡Hola! ¿Cómo estás?* (Hello! How are you?)
- *Hola, estoy buscando la embajada* (Hello, I'm looking for the embassy)

Hola is the most basic, most general greeting. But in Spanish you have several other options. You can say *buenos días* (or *buenas tardes*, or *buenas noches*). These are the equivalents to our "good morning", "good afternoon", "good evening" and "good night". They are almost always appropriate, as long as you're using them at the correct time of the day. Let's see them in action:

- *Buenos días, ¿cómo está usted?* (Good morning, how are you?)
- *Buenas tardes. ¿Esta es la oficina de Guillermo?* (Good afternoon. Is this Guillermo's office?)
- *Buenas noches, Mara. Qué bueno encontrarte aquí.* (Good evening, Mara. How nice to run into you here)

There's a slight difference between the languages here: while English makes a distinction between "good evening" and "good night", Spanish uses *buenas noches* in both cases. Besides these formulas, which depend on the time of the day, we have a lot of questions that work as conversation openers. Here are some of them:

- *¿Qué tal?* (What's up?)
- *¿Cómo estás?* (How are you?)
- *¿Cómo te va?* (How are you doing?)

And you also have to learn to say goodbye, of course. The word *adiós* is the most common one; you can also find the diminutive (more informal) version of this word, *adiosito*, and *chao* ("bye"). But there are also a lot of formulas that include, in some way or another, the words *hasta* ("until") and *nos vemos* ("see you"). Here you can see some examples:

- *Adiós. Nos vemos mañana.* (Goodbye. See you tomorrow)
- *Hasta la próxima.* (Until next time)
- *Hasta pronto.* (See you soon)
- *¡Adiosito! Cuídate.* (Bye-bye! Take care)
- *Chao, Carlos.* (Bye, Carlos)

Disculpas y perdón

Many times, especially if you're interrupting someone who is busy, you'll have to say something like "excuse me" before adding anything else. This is a good way of starting a conversation if you, for example, need to ask a question. And, as we're being polite here, we can also add "sorry".

In Spanish, "excuse me" can be translated as *discúlpame* or *disculpe* (more on the difference between these two conjugations of the verb *disculpar* later in this same chapter). *Perdón* is the usual way of saying "sorry". Let's see them in action:

- *Disculpe, ¿esta es la calle Zapata?* (Excuse me, is this Zapata street?)
- *Perdón, fue un accidente.* (Sorry, it was an accident)

Por favor y gracias

"Thank you" and "please", the magic words! Of course, they have Spanish equivalents. They are "*por favor*" and "*gracias*".

- *Una cerveza, por favor.* (A beer, please)
- *Gracias por tu ayuda.* (Thank you for your help)

The Present Tense

Ok, it's time to make our first grammar stop. We'll talk a little bit about the present tense or, in Spanish, *el tiempo presente*. Spanish verbs change a lot depending on which person you are using; the verb *amar* ("to love"), for example, has a first person singular form, a second person singular form, and so on.

This person can be thought of as the one *doing* the action. If *I* do the action, the verb takes a certain form; if *you* do the action, it takes another one; if *they* do it, it takes a third one. In English, verbs don't change much depending on who is doing the action, but, in Spanish, they do.

In English and in Spanish, we can say that there are three main persons: the first one, that includes the speaker; the second one, that includes the listener; and the third one, that refers to something or someone that is not participating in the conversation. They can also be divided between singular and plural—both "I" and "we" include me, but one is singular and the other one is plural.

If we put all that in a chart, we'll end up with something like this:

	Singular		Plural	
Language	English	Spanish	English	Spanish
First person	I	*Yo*	We	*Nosotros/nosotras*
Second person	You	*Tú/usted*	You	*Ustedes*
Third person	He/She	*Él/ella*	They	*Ellos/ellas*

We now know what the different persons are, but... why did we want to know that? Do you remember? I'll give you a hint: because, in Spanish, verbs are conjugated, i.e., they change, according to who is doing the action. Something similar happens in English, but it's limited to the third person singular: we say "I **think**", but then we say "She **thinks**". In Spanish, this variation is much more widespread.

Luckily, most of the verbs are regular. This means that they fall into one of three conjugations, depending on how their infinitive form (the non-conjugated form of the verb) ends. We have three possible endings: AR, ER, and IR. Thus, for regular verbs the root of the verb remains the same; the only thing that changes is the last part. Seems complicated? Don't worry, it'll be easier after you take a look at this table.

		Amar ("to love")	*Temer* ("to fear")	*Partir* ("to leave")
I	*Yo*	*am**o***	*tem**o***	*part**o***
You	*Tú (informal)*	*am**as***	*tem**es***	*part**es***
	Usted (formal)	*am**a***	*tem**e***	*part**e***
He/she	*Él/ella*	*am**a***	*tem**e***	*part**e***
We	*Nosotros/ nosotras*	*am**amos***	*tem**emos***	*part**imos***
You	*Ustedes*	*am**an***	*tem**en***	*part**en***
They	*Ellos/ellas*	*am**an***	*tem**en***	*part**en***

On this table, we have three model verbs: *amar* ("to love"), *temer* ("to fear") and *partir* ("to leave"). All regular verbs fall into one of these free conjugations. So, for example, if you want to use the verb "to run", you'll have to conjugate the verb *corter* accordingly, using the *temer* model, because it ends in ER.

But we also have irregular verbs. The two most important ones are *ser* and *estar*. Both of them can be translated as "to be", but in Spanish they don't mean exactly the same. *Ser* is used for permanent attributes, whereas *estar* is used for temporary states. It's the difference between being tall and being happy: if you're tall, you'll always be tall. If you're happy, well, you won't feel that way all the time..

Here we have a table with the conjugations of *ser* and *estar*:

		Ser ("to be")	*Estar* ("to be")
I	*Yo*	*soy*	*estoy*
You	*Tú (informal)*	*eres*	*estás*
You	*Usted (formal)*	*es*	*está*
He/she	*Él/ella*	*es*	*está*
We	*Nosotros/ nosotras*	*somos*	*estamos*
You	*Ustedes*	*son*	*están*
They	*Ellos/ellas*	*son*	*están*

Tú y usted

Do you remember when we talked about the difference between *discúlpame* and *disculpe*? We said that we would talk more about that later. Well, that time has come.

We said a little more about that subject when we saw the present tense. As you surely noticed, in Spanish there are two different forms for the second person singular: *tú* and *usted*. The difference between these two lies in the degree of formality. *Tú* is casual and informal; *usted* is formal, and it's used mainly when you want to highlight your respect for the person you are talking to. It's very common to use *usted* with older people, for example, or with people that have authority, like a police officer.

Verbs that go alongside *tú* and *usted* have to be conjugated differently. We also saw that in the past section. In Spanish, we say *tú amas* and *usted ama*. This difference can look difficult, but there is a trick: the form associated with *usted* is, in regular verbs, identical to the form associated with *él/ella*, the third person singular. If you don't believe me, go back to the table and check it out yourself!

¿Cuál es tu nombre?

We are now in the last section of the theory part of this chapter. Here, we're going to focus on the most important part of a conversation with a stranger: introducing ourselves. Because you want to be able to say your name, don't you?

There are three main ways of talking about names in Spanish:

- *Mi nombre es Susana.* (My name is Susana)
- *Él se llama José María.* (He's called José María)
- *Usted es Clara, ¿verdad?* (You are Clara, am I right?)

Reversely, you can also ask for names using these formulas:

- *¿Cuál es tu nombre?* (What's your name?)
- *¿Cómo se llama ella?* (How is she called?)
- *¿Quién es usted?* (Who are you?)

Just like in English, this last question can sound a bit rude, but it can be softened with the correct intonation.

Key Takeaways

- In Spanish, there are a lot of ways of saying "hello", like *hola, buenos días,* or *¿qué tal?* We also have several options for goodbye, like *adiós, chao, adiosito, hasta luego* and *nos vemos luego.*
- *Disculpa* ("excuse me"), *perdón* ("sorry"), *por favor* ("please") and *gracias* ("thank you") are words associated with politeness and good manners.

- Regarding grammar, we saw how regular verbs are conjugated in the present simple. Besides, we also saw how to conjugate two of the most important irregular verbs: *ser* and *estar*.
- *Tú* and *usted* are two different forms of the second person singular. The first one is associated with informal and familiar conversations; the latter is used to indicate formality and to show respect.
- Finally, we saw how to introduce ourselves and how to ask for other people's names.

This is a nice summary of the main topics of this chapter. You are now able to start a conversation, although... it's still a bit difficult to keep it going, isn't it? At least for now. But there's no need to worry, the next chapter is going to help you with that: we're going to talk about questions! Keep on reading if you want to know more. However, before moving on, let's check what we've seen so far.

Chapter Exercises

1. Fill in the blanks in this dialogue with one of these words:

   luego, estás, hola, tú, perdón, gracias.

   A: _____, Mario, ¿cómo _____?

   B: Bien, ¿y _____?

   A: Muy bien. Escucha, _____, pero no tengo mucho

tiempo. ¿Podemos hablar más tarde?

B: No hay problema, Joaquín.

A: Muchas _____. ¡Hasta _____!

2. Conjugate the verbs in brackets in the present tense.

   a. Ana _____ (correr) todas las mañanas.

   b. Nosotros _____ (estar) perdidos.

   c. Ellos _____ (cocinar) muy bien.

   d. Yo _____ (salir) seguido.

3. Decide whether the following statements are true or false. Correct the false ones.

   a. *Usted* is used in formal contexts.

   b. *Estar* is a regular verb.

   c. *Adiosito* is a formal greeting.

   d. *Ser* means "to be".

4. Let's see a bit of grammar. Which of the following sentences is grammatically correct?

   a. ¡Buenos días! Mi nombre está Gustavo.

   b. ¡Bueno día! Mi nombre está Gustavo.

c. ¡Buenos días! Mi nombre es Gustavo.

d. ¡Bueno día! Mi nombre es Gustavo.

5. In the next sentences, choose from the words in brackets to fill in the blanks.

a. (Tú/usted) _____ es muy interesante.

b. Los perros no _____ (habla/hablan).

c. ¡Justo lo que necesito! Muchas _____
(disculpas/gracias).

d. Yo _____ (soy/estoy) triste.

6. Match each question with its possible answers.

a. ¿Cuál es tu nombre?   1. Todo bien.

b. ¿Cómo te llamas?   2. Laura, ¿y el tuyo?

c. ¿Cómo estás?   3. María, ¿y tú?

d. ¿Qué tal?   4. Yo estoy bien, ¿y tú?

7. Read the following dialogue and then answer the questions.

A: Disculpe, señora, pero estoy perdido. ¿Puedo hacerle una pregunta, por favor?

B: ¡Buenos días! Pues claro.

A: ¿Cuál es el nombre de esta calle?

B: La calle se llama Madero.

A: ¡Muchas gracias! Ahora solo necesito saber hacia dónde queda la estación de buses.

B: Queda hacia el norte. Yo justo voy en esa dirección. Si quieres, podemos caminar juntos hasta allí.

A: ¡Gracias! Encantado.

B: ¿Cómo te llamas?

A: José, ¿y tú?

B: Ramona.

a. What is B's name?

b. Where is A going?

c. What's the name of the street A and B are currently on?

d. According to the way they talk, who do you think is older, A or B?

8. Which of the following sentences is grammatically incorrect?

a. Me llamo Lucía y soy pastelera.

b. Discúlpame, ¿puedo pasar?

c. Usted tienes un reloj muy bonito.

d. Muchas gracias por su ayuda, usted es muy amable.

9. Fill in the blanks with the correct conjugation of the verb *ser* or the verb *estar*.

a. Esteban _____ maestro de grado.

b. Yo _____ cansado hoy.

c. Ustedes _____ un mejor equipo.

d. Ellas _____ muy bien preparadas para el examen.

10. Correct the sentences which have verbs in the wrong conjugation.

a. Los estudiantes está callados dentro del aula.

b. Tú tienes un nombre muy original.

c. Nosotros saben la respuesta correcta.

d. Yo soy profesor de química.

Answer Key

1.

A: Hola, Mario, ¿cómo estás?

B: Bien, ¿y tú?

A: Muy bien. Escucha, perdón, pero no tengo mucho tiempo. ¿Podemos hablar más tarde?

B: No hay problema, Joaquín. ¡Hasta luego!

2.

a. Ana corre todas las mañanas.

b. Nosotros estamos perdidos.

c. Ellos cocinan muy bien.

d. Yo salgo seguido.

3.

a. True.

b. False. *Estar* is an irregular verb.

c. False. *Adiosito* is an informal way of saying goodbye.

d. True

4.

c. ¡Buenos días! Mi nombre es Gustavo.

5.

    a. Usted es muy interesante.

    b. Los perros no hablan.

    c. ¡Justo lo que necesito! Muchas gracias.

    d. Yo estoy triste.

6.

    a. ¿Cuál es tu nombre? 2. Laura, ¿y el tuyo?

    b. ¿Cómo te llamas? 3. María, ¿y tú?

    c. ¿Cómo estás? 4. Yo estoy bien, ¿y tú?

    d. ¿Qué tal? 1. Todo bien.

7.

    a. Ramona

    b. The bus station.

    c. Madero.

    d. B, Ramona.

8.

    c. Usted tienes un reloj muy bonito.

9.

    a. Esteban es maestro de grado.

    b. Yo estoy cansado hoy.

    c. Ustedes son un mejor equipo.

    d. Ellas están muy bien preparadas para el examen.

10.

    a. Los estudiantes están callados dentro del aula.

    c. Nosotros sabemos la respuesta correcta.

Chapter 2: Questions in Mexico

¿Qué haría yo sin lo absurdo y lo fugaz?

- Frida Kahlo

Curiosity drives the world. It's one of the strongest forces in human nature; a propensity for asking, questioning and wondering has defined the lives of many of the greatest scientists, artists and explorers in history. From Aristotle to Darwin, the capacity to ask questions has always been fundamental. We ask, and therefore we know.

You may not want to discover something as relevant as evolution; you may be, after all, on a holiday, or traveling for work. But you don't need to be a scientist to ask questions. Every conversation has plenty of them—or at least every good one. Remember: if you're not asking questions, that means you're only talking about yourself. And that is not exactly entertaining.

So, in this chapter, we're going to work precisely on that. We're going to turn you into a questioning machine. Of course, that means you'll need some preparation, both in questioning and grammar. So, in this chapter, we're going to talk about:

- interrogative words in Spanish
- gender and number in nouns
- agreement between nouns and other words
- yes or no questions
- questions tags

Interrogative Pronouns and Interrogative Adverbs

In English, we have a set of words we use in questions. They are known as the wh- words, because all but one start with those two letters; they are, of course, "what", "why", "when", "where", "who", "which" and "how". In Spanish, we have very close equivalents: the interrogative pronouns and interrogative adverbs.

Of course, as it often happens, the equivalence is not exactly one-to-one, so we should make a few clarifications. We should also, for the sake of clarity, differentiate between the interrogative pronouns and the interrogative adverbs, but that will be easier after you know them. So, first of all, let's make a list with the words, their English counterparts, and a few examples for each one:

1. *qué*: what
   ¿Qué tienes en la mano? (What do you have in your hand?)
   ¿Qué día es hoy? (What day is today?)
2. *quién*: who
   ¿Quién es el responsable de esto? (Who is responsible for

this?)

¿Quién tiene hambre? (Who is hungry?)

3. *cuándo*: when

   ¿Cuándo llegamos a la playa? (When do we get to the beach?)

   ¿Cuándo sale el tren? (When does the train leave?)

4. *dónde*: where

   ¿Dónde está Pepe? (Where is Pepe?)

   ¿Dónde puedo comprar comida? (Where can I buy food?)

5. *por qué*: why

   ¿Por qué vuelan los pájaros? (Why do birds fly?)

   ¿Por qué siempre llegas tarde? (Why do you always arrive late?)

6. *cuál*: which/what

   ¿Cuál playera prefieres? (Which t-shirt do you prefer?)

   ¿Cuál es tu nombre? (What is your name?)

7. *cómo*: how

   ¿Cómo abres esto? (How do you open this?)

   ¿Cómo va el partido? (How is the match going?)

8. *cuánto*: how much/how many

   ¿Cuánto cuesta esa chaqueta? (How much does that jacket cost?)

   ¿Cuántos invitados vienen a la fiesta? (How many guests are coming to the party?)

It doesn't look that hard, does it? I thought so. Anyways, we still have a few things to discuss. The first and most obvious one is that, in Spanish, questions have an opening question mark, "¿", and a closing one, "?". You probably already noticed it, but maybe you don't know what its function is. English questions have a different word order from English statements, so you can tell something written down is a question even before you get to the closing question mark. Spanish questions, on the other hand, have the same word order as affirmative statements. In Speaking, you can tell you are being asked a question by intonation; in writing, the opening question mark tells you that you are going to read a question.

Now, let's talk about the difference between interrogative adverbs and interrogative pronouns. First of all, we're going to put all the words into the two categories; then, we're going to talk about what each category means.

- Interrogative pronouns: *qué, quién, cuál, cuánto.*
- Interrogative adverbs: *dónde, cómo, cuándo.*

As you can see, *por qué* is not on this list. Why? Well, basically because it's not a single word. It's a sequence made up by the interrogative pronoun *qué* and the preposition *por*. But that's not what's important here.

In fact, the difference between interrogative pronouns and interrogative adverbs is important only for one reason. Interrogative pronouns, like almost all pronouns, change; adverbs don't. In Spanish, that change is called *concordancia* ("agreement"), and it's related to number and gender. But we will need a whole new section for that.

Agreement: Number and Gender

Let's start from the beginning: in Spanish, nouns have number (singular or plural) and gender (masculine or feminine). For example, *mesa* ("table") is a feminine and singular noun; *aviones* ("planes") is masculine and plural noun; *rata* ("rat") is feminine and singular; and so on and so forth.

"Wait a minute", you may be thinking. "I get the number part. I get the singular and the plural, it's the same as in English. But, what about *gender*? Does *every* noun have gender?"

I'm glad you asked. In Spanish, as in many other languages, nouns have an assigned gender. This affects *all* nouns, not only the ones referring to people and animals. Most of them are invariable, that is, they are always either masculine or feminine. It's not like with number, where you can change a singular noun to make it plural. Besides people and animals, most nouns just have to work with the gender they have. And—I'm sorry for this—gender assignment it's mostly random. You'll find no pattern. Whenever you learn a new noun, you need to learn it together with its gender.

Why is the gender of a noun important? Because of agreement. If the noun is masculine and singular, that means that a lot of other words in the sentence—mainly adjectives and pronouns—are going to be masculine and singular too. They change together; they are linked.

Let's see it with a few examples. *Caballo* ("horse") is a masculine noun; *yegua* ("mare") is a feminine noun. That means that you'll have to say *lindo caballo* ("nice horse") and *linda yegua* ("nice mare"). The adjective, *lindo/a*, has to agree with the noun.

But most nouns don't respond to a real-world difference like the one we can find between a horse and a mare. A table is just a table. Why do we have to worry about the gender of *mesa* if there is no **meso*? (Note that in this book—and in many other language books—the asterisk is used to indicate that a word doesn't exist or that a phrase is agrammatical.)

Well, again, because of agreement. *Mesa* ("table") is a feminine noun. That means that the words around it, the adjectives and pronouns that modify it, have to be in their feminine form. We'll say *linda mesa*, and not **lindo mesa* or ** lindo meso*.

I'm aware that this sounds a little complicated. And I'm not going to lie: it is—at least at the beginning. But you don't have to incorporate it all at once. Every Spanish student in history has fought against number and gender at first, and, after a few lost battles, most have won. You'll get better at it with practice. After all, remember that Spanish speakers use it all the time! To make it a little easier for you at the beginning, in this book we list all nouns together with their article, so there's no doubt about their gender: *la* is the article for feminine nouns, and *el* is the article for masculine nouns.

Difference Between Interrogative Pronouns and Interrogative Adverbs

Now that we've discussed Spanish gender, let's get back to our subject. In practice, the difference between interrogative pronouns and interrogative adverbs can be summed up in just one sentence: pronouns change, adverbs don't. Basically, this means that interrogative pronouns (*qué, quién, cuál, cuánto*) are affected by agreement, and thus, we have these variations:

- *quién* (singular), *quiénes* (plural)
- *cuál* (singular), *cuáles* (plural)
- *cuánto* (masculine, singular), *cuántos* (masculine, plural), *cuánta* (feminine, singular), *cuántas* (feminine, plural)

Luckily, *qué* doesn't change; it remains the same regardless of the words around it. The same thing happens with adverbs: you say *cómo*, but you can't say **cóma* or **cómos*.

However, if *qué* doesn't change, why is it a pronoun and not an adverb? Well, because it works as a pronoun, that is, it takes the place of a noun. And this is important, because interrogative pronouns change according to the noun they are replacing.

Let's take a minute to talk about this. Do you remember agreement? The variation based on gender and number? Well, these pronouns have to agree with something. That's when the whole "taking the place of a noun" starts to make sense.

It will be clearer with an example. Look:

- *¿Cuánto tiempo tienes?* (How much time do you have?)
- *¿Cuánta plata tienes?* (How much money do you have?)
- *¿Cuántos perros tienes?* (How many dogs do you have?)
- *¿Cuántas casas tienes?* (How many houses do you have?)

In these examples, the interrogative pronoun (*cuánto, cuánta, cuántos, cuantas*) agrees in gender and number with the noun of the sentence: *tiempo* is masculine and singular; *plata* is feminine and singular; *perro* is masculine and singular; and *casas* is feminine and plural. Thus, the interrogative pronoun changes accordingly. Luckily, it's the only interrogative pronoun that has different forms for different genders; with the rest of them you just have to worry about number:

- *¿Quién sabe la respuesta?* (Who knows the answer?)
- *¿Quiénes hicieron la tarea?* (Who did the homework?)
- *¿Cuál es tu perro?* (Which one is your dog?)

- *¿Cuáles prefieres?* (Which ones do you prefer?)

Yes or No Questions

I know, all that grammar was hard. But trust me, all that talk about number, gender and agreement will come in handy in the future. You don't need to learn it by heart; you just have to put a pin on that and have that short section as a reference. And in the meantime, we can keep going.

As we're talking about questions, we should mention the different kinds of questions, right? Open questions, like the ones we ask with interrogative pronouns, are important, but they are not the only ones. We can also find, for example, closed questions, also known as "yes or no questions".

Of course, you already know this type of question. We have them in English, and we use them all the time. Here you have an example:

- Are you hungry?

In Spanish, we'd say something like:

- *¿Tienes hambre?*

Can you spot the main difference between these two? (Yes, that was also a yes or no question; No, I didn't do it on purpose). As we mentioned above, the main difference is that, in Spanish, we don't have to change the word order. The difference between an

Page | 27

affirmative sentence and an interrogative one lies mainly in intonation, on a discreet trend upwards at the end of the utterance.

In English, we say "You are hungry" as an affirmation, and "Are you hungry?" as a question. In Spanish, it's easier than that. *Tienes hambre* and *¿Tienes hambre?* have the same grammar; you just have to pronounce them a little differently when speaking: with an upward intonation. And, when writing, you just need to use the opening and closing question marks.

Question Tags

Sometimes, when we end an affirmative sentence, we suddenly have the urge to make it a question. This sounds complicated, but we actually do it all the time. It's what happens when we say something like "Studying Spanish isn't hard, is it?"

As you can see, that short tag at the end of the sentence is doing a lot of work. In many cases, we can also replace it with a "right?" tag ("Studying Spanish isn't hard, right?"). It's somehow important to notice that we frequently use these questions in a rhetorical way; we don't really expect our interlocutor to answer them. But we still ask them, and we should know how to do it in Spanish.

As we've already seen, in English we use the auxiliary verb in the question tag: "to be", "to do" or another one ("is it?", "isn't it?", "do you?", and so on). In this regard, Spanish is much easier. You just have to add a *¿no?* at the end. Let's see how that works in a few English-to-Spanish translations.

English	Spanish
He's leaving tomorrow, isn't he?	*Él se va mañana, ¿no?*
We're in this together, aren't we?	*Estamos juntas en esto, ¿no?*
You don't really care, do you?	*No te importa, ¿no?*
I am not wrong, am I?	*No estoy equivocado, ¿no?*

You *could* use *¿sí?* instead of *¿no?* in some cases, mainly in affirmative sentences (*Él se va mañana, ¿sí?*) but it sounds a little bit odd.

Key Takeaways

- In Spanish, open questions start with an interrogative pronoun or an interrogative adverb, such as *qué* ("what"), *quién* ("who"), *cuál* ("which/what"), *cuánto* ("how many/how much"), *cómo* ("how"), *dónde* ("where"), *cuándo* ("when") and *por qué* ("why").

- We also have yes or no questions. Unlike English, they are mostly distinguished by intonation. That's why there are no big grammatical changes between the affirmative sentences and the questions: *Tienes frío* ("You're cold") transforms into *¿Tienes frío?* ("Are you cold?").

- Question tags are very simple: just add a *¿no?* at the end of the sentence!
- In Spanish, nouns have number (singular or plural) and gender (masculine or feminine).
- The number and the gender of the noun are very important, because many other words in the sentence are "linked" with them, and change accordingly. That phenomenon is called agreement. That's why we say *El té está frío* ("The tea is cold") and *Las papas están frías* ("The potatoes are cold"), and not **El té está frías* nor **Las papas está frío*.

Until this moment, we mostly saw very basic Spanish structures: verbs in the present tense, questions, and agreement between nouns and adjectives. These grammar patterns are shared between all different Spanish dialects, as they are the underlying structure of the language. Well, for the most part. Now that we have some sense of how Spanish works, we can do a big dive into the differences between European Spanish and Mexican Spanish. Most of them have to do with vocabulary, but you'll find there are some grammatical intricacies.

That's going to be the subject of our next chapter. But, before delving into it, we have to do a fast check on what we've learned in chapter 2!

Chapter Exercises

1. Fill in the blanks with one of the following words: *cuánto, qué, cómo, cuál.*

   a. ¿_____ te llamas?

   b. ¿_____ es tu comida favorita?

   c. ¿_____ quieres hacer?

   d. ¿_____ cuesta este libro?

2. Match each question on the left with an answer on the right.

   a. ¿Cuántos años tienes?   1. Porque ya pasó demasiado tiempo.

   b. ¿Cuándo termina la película?   2. A las nueve y media.

   c. ¿Cómo volveremos de la fiesta? 3. En taxi.

   d. ¿Por qué no le dices la verdad? 4. Treinta y dos.

3. In the next questions, choose from the words in brackets to fill in the blanks.

   a. ¿_____ (cuántas/cuántos) perros tienes?

   b. ¿_____ (quién/quiénes) hacen ejercicio todas las semanas?

c. ¿_____ (qué/cuál) me quieres decir?

d. ¿_____ (dónde/cuándo) está la estación?

4. Which of the following sentences is grammatically correct?

   a. ¿Cuántos tienes perros?

   b. Ese es Tomás, ¿no?

   c. ¿Quiénes sale esta noche?

   d. La playa es muy bonito, ¿no?

5. Decide whether the following statements are true or false. Correct the false ones.

   a. In Spanish, all nouns have an assigned gender: masculine or feminine.

   b. Interrogative adverbs change to agree with the noun.

   c. Yes or no questions have the same word order as affirmative sentences.

   d. The gender of nouns is never randomly assigned.

6. Which of the following sentences is grammatically incorrect?

   a. ¿Dónde guardas el azúcar?

   b. Tú estudiaste astronomía, ¿no?

c. ¿Nos vemos mañana?

d. ¿Cuántos cuestan dos boletos?

7. Fill in the blanks in the following dialogue with one of these words: *aquí, cuánto, no, alojamiento, acogedor, cuándo, nueve.*

A: ¿_____ sale el próximo tren?

B: Mañana a las _____ de la mañana.

A: Eso significa que tendré que pasar la noche aquí,

¿_____?

B: Si necesita un _____, yo puedo ayudarlo.

A: ¿Tiene alguno cerca de _____? Estoy cansado de caminar.

B: Hay uno a dos cuadras, un hotel muy _____.

A: ¿_____ cuesta la noche?

B: Diez dólares.

8. Fill in the blanks with the correct form of the adjective *lindo*, taking agreement into account.

a. Qué _____ pájaro.

b. Esas montañas son muy _____.

c. Recorrimos unos bosques muy _____.

d. Espero que mañana tengamos una _____ mañana.

9. Correct the adjectives that don't agree with the noun.

    a. Los edificios más altas están en el centro de la ciudad.

    b. Mañana tendremos un día caluroso.

    c. Los pasajes caros no valen la pena.

    d. Hoy tengo un plan maravillosos.

10. Answer these questions in your own words.

    a. ¿Cuál es tu pasatiempo?

    b. ¿Dónde naciste?

    c. ¿Cómo es tu casa?

    d. ¿Cuál es tu película favorita?

Answer Key

1.

a. ¿Cómo te llamas?

b. ¿Cuál es tu comida favorita?

c. ¿Qué quieres hacer?

d. ¿Cuánto cuesta este libro?

2.

a. ¿Cuántos años tienes? 4. Treinta y dos

b. ¿Cuándo termina la película? 2. A las nueve y media.

c. ¿Cómo volveremos de la fiesta? 3. En taxi.

d. ¿Por qué no le dices la verdad? 1. Porque ya pasó demasiado tiempo.

3.

a. ¿Cuántos perros tienes?

b. ¿Quiénes hacen ejercicio todas las semanas?

c. ¿Qué me quieres decir?

d. ¿Dónde está la estación?

4.

b. Ese es Tomás, ¿no?

5.

a. True.

b. False. Interrogative adverbs dont' change.

c. True.

d. The gender of many nouns is randomly assigned.

6.

d. ¿Cuántos cuestan dos boletos?

7.

A: ¿Cuándo sale el próximo tren?

B: Mañana a las nueve de la mañana.

A: Eso significa que tendré que pasar la noche aquí, ¿no?

B: Si necesita un alojamiento, yo puedo ayudarlo.

A: ¿Tiene alguno cerca de aquí? Estoy cansado de caminar.

B: Hay uno a dos cuadras, un hotel muy acogedor.

A: ¿Cuánto cuesta la noche?

B: Diez dólares.

8.

a. Qué lindo pájaro.

b. Esas montañas son muy lindas.

c. Recorrimos unos bosques muy lindos.

d. Espero que mañana tengamos una linda mañana.

9.

a. Los edificios más altos están en el centro de la ciudad.

d. Hoy tengo un plan maravilloso.

Chapter 3: Mexican Spanish vs. European Spanish

No acabarán mis flores,

no cesarán mis cantos.

Yo cantor los elevo,

se reparten, se esparcen.

Aun cuando las flores

se marchitan y amarillecen,

serán llevadas allá,

al interior de la casa

del ave de plumas de oro.

- Nezahualcóyotl, the "Poet King"

Spanish is one of the most popular languages in the world. From the hot African coasts of Equatorial Guinea to the icy Andean mountains in Argentina, Spanish spreads across the world and through more than 500 million speakers. And that is if you only count *native* speakers.

With these many speakers comes variation. We can't expect all these people to talk the same, especially when they're so far apart from each other. Living in different corners of the world means being exposed to different stimuli, migrations and languages, and all that most definitely impacts vocabulary and grammar. Andean Spanish speakers—mostly located in Peru and Bolivia—have a very close relationship with Quechua and Aymara, two indigenous languages that many people speak natively. Rioplatense Spanish, down South, has a pronunciation that very closely resembles the one of Italian, and that is due to massive Italian immigration at the beginning of the 20th century.

But we're not here to talk about Andean Spanish or Rioplatense Spanish, or any of the many Spanish varieties you can find out there. In this book, we're interested in only one of them: Mexican Spanish.

Mexican Spanish, of course, has its own intricacies. It's the most spoken dialect of the Spanish language, even more than European Spanish (that's not a surprise if you take into account that Mexico is the most populous Spanish-speaking country). Of course, not all people in Mexico speak in the same way. It's a very big country—the 13th biggest in the world—which means that speakers in the Yucatan Peninsula are very far apart from the ones in the Sonoran Desert.

However, we can find shared patterns and common elements. The thing is that it's difficult to underline them if we don't have something to compare them to. Differences are not differences if they are all we know. That's why, in this chapter, we're going to compare Mexican Spanish with European Spanish, which is the most commonly taught variation of the language. If you've studied even a little Spanish at any point in your life, you'll probably feel that this is familiar; and if you haven't, and this is your first approach to the language, you'll be able to detect the difference you'll surely have with other Spanish speakers.

That's why, in this chapter, we're going to focus on:

- The Nahuatl influence on Mexican Spanish.
- Mexicanisms: Spanish words that are only used in Mexico.
- The difference between *ustedes* and *vosotros*, both forms of the second person plural.
- The imperative in Mexican Spanish.

Nahuatl Influence

Nahuatl is not the only indigenous language spoken in Mexico, but, for various reasons—location, political power, and importance—it's the most influential one. It was spoken by the Aztecs, the pre-Columbian imperial power of the region, and it's still spoken today by around 1.5 million people.

Before the Conquest of Mexico, Nahuatl was the *lingua franca* of Central America. That means that, although it wasn't everybody's native language, it was still the most used one. Many people around the region spoke even a little bit of Nahuatl. When the Spaniards took power, they had to communicate with a very culturally diverse group of nations. In many cases, they used Nahuatl.

That's why many of the words that refer to things exclusively found in that region are taken from Nahuatl. Remember: when the Spaniards arrived, they had never seen an avocado, or a tomato, or a cocoa bean. They had to find names for all those things in their own language, Spanish. And, quite logically, they borrowed the names that were already in use: Nahuatl names.

In those cases, the Spanish word that came from Nahuatl is frequently used both in Mexican Spanish and European Spanish. After all, in Spain they just didn't have a way of calling those things; the language loan was not "competing" against any existing word. But not all Nahuatl vocabulary comes from exclusively Mexican things.

In some cases, there was a redundancy. There were things that existed in both cultures, and, quite consequently, there were ways to call them in both languages. A few times, in Mexico, that redundancy was resolved in favor of the Nahuatl word. In those cases, that loan is mostly confined to Mexican Spanish; European Spanish speakers have their own, different word with the same meaning.

But enough with linguistic history. It's thrilling, I know, but we can't keep going in this direction. We have, of course, to make a vocabulary list of Mexican words derived from Nahuatl. Remember that some of these words have an equivalent in European Spanish, which people in Spain use more frequently, and some are shared by both dialects. Here, enjoy!

Mexican Spanish word derived from Nahuatl	English translation	European Spanish equivalent (if any)
el aguacate	avocado	-
el jitomate	tomato	*tomate*
el cacahuate	peanut	*cacahuete*
el chocolate	chocolate	-
el cacao	cocoa	-
el elote	corn, maize ear	*maíz*
el guajolote	turkey	*pavo*
el cuate, la cuate	friend	*colega, tío*

el chicle	gum	–
el hule	rubber	–
el papalote	kite	*cometa*
apapachar	to hug and touch affectionately	*abrazar* (it's not exactly the same)
el popote	straw	*pajilla*
la tlapalería	hardware store	*ferretería*

Mexicanisms

Mexican Spanish has a lot of influences. There are a lot of words that Mexicans use that are not common in other Spanish dialects; some, as we've already seen, come from Nahuatl, but not all of them. Many are loans from other indigenous languages, or even from English (being so close to the United States has favored that kind of linguistic exchange). There are even some words that can be considered "archaisms", in the sense that they were common in Spain many centuries ago, but fell out of use everywhere but in Mexico.

This doesn't mean speakers from other dialects don't understand them. Spanish speakers from all over the world understand each other just fine, in the same way an American, a South African and an Australian do. The differences can be easily explained, and they don't produce anything but small—and often fun—misunderstandings.

That said, we're back to where we were with words derived from Nahuatl: we need a list. That's why here you'll find some—but not all—Mexicanism, with their English and European Spanish translations. In this case, we're also going to have a few examples, because not all the words are nouns (which are easier to understand without context).

Mexicanism	Example	English translation	English translation of the example	European Spanish equivalent (if any)
las agujetas	*Tienes las agujetas desatadas.*	shoelaces	Your shoelaces are untied.	*los cordones*
la alberca	*¿Nos metemos en la alberca?*	pool	Do you want to get in the pool?	*la piscina*
el antro	*Conozco un antro muy bueno cerca de aquí.*	bar	I know a really good bar near here.	*el bar*

la banqueta	Caminemos por la banqueta de la sombra.	sidewalk	Let's walk on the sidewalk in the shade.	la acera
bonche (de)	En el refrigerador hay bonche de comida.	many, a lot	In the fridge there is a lot of food.	mucho/a
la colonia	Ese bar queda en la colonia Roma.	neighborhood (specially in Mexico City)	That bar is in the Roma neighborhood.	el barrio
la cruda	Todavía tengo una cruda terrible.	hangover	I'm still terribly hungover.	la resaca
el chamaco, la chamaca	¿Quién es ese chamaco?	kid	Who's that kid?	el chaval, la chavala
la chamarra	Esta chamarra es muy abrigada.	jacket	This jacket is very warm.	la chaqueta
chambear	Mañana me levanto temprano para	to work	Tomorrow I wake up early for work.	trabajar

	chambear.			
la chela	Una chela fría, por favor.	beer	A cold beer, please.	la cerveza
fregar	Él me quiere fregar, yo lo sé.	to annoy	He wants to annoy me, I know it.	fastidiar
el güero, la güera	Él es muy güero, no puede estar al sol.	blond	He's very blond, he can't be under the sun.	el rubio, la rubia
el güey	Oye, güey, ¿cómo te llamas?	guy, dude	Hey, dude, what's your name?	el tío, el colega
el huarache	Necesito unos huaraches nuevos.	sandals	I need new sandals.	la sandalia
la lana	Préstame lana, por favor.	money	Lend me some money, please.	el dinero, la plata
el lonche	Quiero un lonche de jamón y queso.	lunch, sandwich	I want a ham and cheese sandwich.	el almuerzo, el sándwich
padrísimo/ a	La película	great, amazing	The movie is great.	increíble, muy

	está padrísima.			bueno
platicar	Platicamos toda la noche.	to talk	We talked all night.	hablar, conversar
la playera	Esta playera me queda gigante.	t-shirt	This t-shirt is too big for me.	la camiseta
la torta	En ese lugar hacen unas tortas padrísimas.	sandwich	In that place they made great sandwiches.	el sándwich, el bocadillo

Ustedes vs. Vosotros

In the first chapter, when we discussed the present tense, we talked about the different persons: first person singular (*yo*), first person plural (*nosotras/nosotros*), second person singular (*tú, usted*), and so on. If you studied Spanish in the past—European Spanish, that is—you probably noticed that, in the second person plural, we used *ustedes* and not *vosotros/vosotras*. Well, that wasn't a mistake. The use of *ustedes* over *vosotros/vosotras* is one of the key differences between Mexican Spanish and European Spanish.

This affects more than the personal pronoun; it's not as easy as changing one word for another. In fact, we're talking about a whole different verb conjugation.

Let's do a quick recap of the first chapter, in which we discussed the present tense. Spanish verbs tend to vary a great deal according to who is doing the action. This variation lies in the ending of the verb, in the last few letters. The idea is that, by looking at the verb ending and taking into account the context, you can more or less identify who is doing the action: whether it's the speaker, the listener, or a third person not taking part in the conversation.

That said, let's get back to where we started this section: the difference between *ustedes* and *vosotros*. Both pronouns refer to a second person plural; they are the equivalent to our plural "you". But they have different conjugations—verbs conjugated in these two pronouns end in different ways.—Here you can see a table with examples from the three Spanish endings, AR, ER and IR:

	Amar	*Temer*	*Partir*
Ustedes	*aman*	*temen*	*parten*
Vosotros/vosotras	*amáis*	*teméis*	*partís*

In Mexico, as in most Latin American countries, people use *ustedes*. *Vosotros/vosotras* is a feature of European Spanish. And this, which could be a little complicated, is in fact good news, because verbs are easier to conjugate when you're using *ustedes*. Why? Well, because you use the same ending as with *ellos/ellas* ("they"). Let's take a look:

	Amar	*Temer*	*Partir*
Nosotros	am**amos**	tem**emos**	part**imos**
Ustedes	am**an**	tem**en**	part**en**
Ellos/ellas	am**an**	tem**en**	part**en**

There you have it! One conjugation less to worry about.

¡Ándale!

If you're familiar with Mexican Spanish, you've probably heard expressions that sound like *¡Ándale!* ("Go!"), *¡Córrele!* ("Run!") or *¡Muévanle!* ("Move it!"). These are imperative verbs, that is, verbs conjugated with the sole purpose of giving orders.

We don't really have that in English. Of course, we give orders—some people give too many—but that doesn't really affect the form of the verbs. It's more about intention and intonation than about grammar. However, in Spanish you can give orders just by changing the ending of the verb. That is called *el modo imperativo* ("the imperative mood").

Of course, as it's an order, we can only give it to our listener, right? So we actually just need the second person. Here is how it looks:

	Amar	*Temer*	*Partir*
Tú	*ama*	*teme*	*parte*
Ustedes	*amen*	*teman*	*partan*

Mexican Spanish speakers use this conjugation, but they frequently add a little twist. It's the *-le* at the end of the word that we saw, at the beginning of the section, in *ándale* and *muévanle*. In those cases, the standard version would be *anda* and *muevan*. But Mexican Spanish speakers like to add a little extra to their orders.

There are grammatical reasons for that *-le*; in Spanish, it's frequently associated with objects, both direct and indirect. But we're not writing a Spanish grammar book here. For now, it's enough that you become familiar with that strange termination, in case you hear it. If you need some extra clarity, you can see here a few more examples:

- *¡Quítale, que no puedo caminar!* (Move it, I can't walk!)
- *¡Ya párale, haces mucho ruido!* (Stop it, you are making too much noise!)

Key Takeaways

- Mexican Spanish has a lot of words with a Nahuatl origin, like *aguacate* or *elote*.

- There are also a lot of mexicanisms, words that are used almost exclusively in Mexico, like *las agujetas*, *el chamaco* or *la playera*.
- Mexican Spanish favors the *ustedes* conjugation over the *vosotros*, the one that's used in European Spanish.
- Imperative, in Mexican Spanish, usually comes with a little extra: a -*le* termination.

In the next chapter, we are going to learn how to talk about jobs and careers in Mexican Spanish. But, first, let's do some exercises on what we've just seen. Are you ready?

Chapter Exercises

1. Transform these verbs conjugated in the second person plural *vosotros/vosotras* to verbs conjugated in the second person plural *ustedes*.
   a. Vosotros llamáis. Ustedes _____.
   b. Vosotras corréis. Ustedes _____.
   c. Vosotras salís. Ustedes _____.
   d. Vosotros bailáis. Ustedes _____.
2. Fill in the blanks with one of the following words: *elote, popote, tlapalería, papalote*.
   a. Ve a la _____ a buscar algunos tornillos.
   b. Compré una botella de soda y vino sin _____.

c. ¿Vamos al parque a volar un _____?

d. Los aztecas usaban _____ en muchas de sus recetas.

3. Which of the following sentences is grammatically correct and makes sense?

    a. Ustedes sabéis la verdad.

    b. Tienes las albercas desatadas.

    c. Él es mi cuate, nos conocemos desde la escuela.

    d. Este cruda es de lo peor.

4. Conjugate the verbs in brackets in the correct tense.

    a. Nosotros no _____ (saber) la respuesta.

    b. Ella _____ (ser) la mejor jugadora del equipo.

    c. ¿Ustedes _____ (querer) terminar temprano?

    d. ¡_____ (cerrar) la puerta, José!

5. Match each question on the left with an answer on the right.

    a. ¿Quieres una chela?   3. Las de pollo, sin dudas.

    b. ¿Necesitas algo del súper?   1. ¡Sí! Helada.

    c. ¿Qué tortas prefieres?   4. En la colonia Condesa.

    d. ¿Dónde vives ahora?   2. Unos jitomates
    maduros, por favor.

6. Which of the following sentences is grammatically incorrect. Rewrite it correctly.

    a. ¿Qué quieren de cenar?

    b. Ponte un chamarra, que hace frío.

    c. Ayer fui a ver un concierto padrísimo.

    d. Ustedes platicáis todo el día.

7. Decide whether the following statements are true or false. Correct the false ones.

a. Mexican Spanish is influenced by Nahuatl.

b. There are no grammatical differences between European Spanish and Mexican Spanish.

c. Spanish speakers around the world have a hard time understanding each other.

d. Mexicans use some words that Spanish people stopped using a long time ago.

8. Fill in the blanks in the following dialogue with one of these words: *estamos, chambear, lana, pueden, estabas.*

A: No quiero _____ mañana, Juan. Estoy harto.

B: ¿Por qué? Creí que _____ contento.

A: Estoy contento con la _____.

B: Eso es bastante. En mi trabajo _____ en la miseria.

A: Pero ustedes _____ trabajar desde casa. Y tienen horario flexible.

9. In the next sentences, choose from the words in brackets to fill in the blanks.

a. Oye, chamaco, _____ (pásame/pasas) la sal.

b. Ustedes no _____ (tenéis/tienen) idea de lo que hablan.

c. ¿Tienes esta _____ (playera/playa) en una talla más grande?

d. _____ (Apapachan/Apapachame), por favor.

10. Put the following dialogue in order.

 1. Tacos al pastor. Estoy muy hambriento.

 2. ¿Ustedes ya saben qué van a ordenar en el antro?

 3. Ni que lo digas, yo hoy no llegué al lonche.

 4. Unas tortas de pollo y aguacate. ¿Y tú?

Answer Key

1.

 a. Vosotros llamáis. Ustedes llaman.

 b. Vosotros corréis. Ustedes corren.

 c. Vosotros salís. Ustedes salen.

 d. Vosotros bailáis. Ustedes bailan.

2.

 a. Ve a la tlapalería a buscar algunos tornillos.

 b. Compré una botella de soda y vino sin popote.

 c. ¿Vamos al parque a volar un papalote?

 d. Los aztecas usaban elote en muchas de sus recetas.

3.

 c. Él es mi cuate, nos conocemos desde la escuela.

4.

 a. Nosotros no sabemos la respuesta.

 b. Ella es la mejor jugadora del equipo.

 c. ¿Ustedes quieren terminar temprano?

 d. ¡Cierra la puerta, José!

5.

    a. ¿Quieres una chela?   1. ¡Sí! Helada.

    b. ¿Necesitas algo del súper?   2. Unos jitomates
maduros, por favor.

    c. ¿Qué tortas prefieres?   3. Las de pollo, sin dudas.

    d. ¿Dónde vives ahora?   4. En la colonia Condesa.

6.

    b. Ponte una chamarra, que hace frío.

    d. Ustedes platican todo el día.

7.

    a. True.

    b. False. There are grammatical differences between
European Spanish and Mexican Spanish, like the use of
vosotros/vosotras in the former and of *ustedes* in the latter.

    c. False. Spanish speakers around the world understand
each other.

    d. True.

8.

    A: No quiero chambear mañana, Juan. Estoy harto.

    B: ¿Por qué? Creí que estabas contento.

    A: Estoy contento con la lana.

    B: Eso es bastante. En mi trabajo estamos en la miseria.

    A: Pero ustedes pueden trabajar desde casa. Y tienen
horario flexible.

9.

   a. Oye, chamaco, pásame la sal.

   b. Ustedes no tienen idea de lo que hablan.

   c. ¿Tienes esta playera en una talla más grande?

   d. Apapáchame, por favor.

10.

   2. ¿Ustedes ya saben qué van a ordenar en el antro?

   4. Unas tortas de pollo y aguacate. ¿Y tú?

   1. Tacos al pastor. Estoy muy hambriento.

   3. Ni que lo digas, yo hoy no llegué al lonche.

Chapter 4: The Wondrous World of Work

El flojo
trabaja dos
veces

- Mexican
proverb

Work is an integral part of human life. It's what makes the world go round, as they say. And it's a vital part of conversation too. People want to know all about other people's jobs, especially if they are strange or risky. What's more interesting than, let's say, a circus acrobat, or an old doll restorer?

But work is not only important as a subject for everyday, casual conversation. Being able to talk about jobs, careers, tasks, pay, and applications is vital as a navigation tool in any country. If you want to find a job in a Spanish-speaking country like Mexico, even if your work is done exclusively in English, this kind of vocabulary would be very helpful. Even more, it's a fundamental part of navigating a city: if you want to be able to find a policeman, a plumber or a doctor.

So that's what we're going to do here. In this chapter, we're going to focus on:

- jobs
- work-related vocabulary
- common dialogues about work
- a little nudge on grammar: the past tense

Let's get started.

Jobs

There is an almost infinite range of professions, crafts and trades. Luckily, you don't have to know them all; we'll give you a strong base, enough to navigate a conversation. Here you'll learn the basics, or at least some of them. After that, you'll build your own vocabulary with time. Remember that experience is the best teacher.

However, there's a little warning: jobs usually have different names in different dialects. In Spain and Mexico, plumber is called *fontanero*, but is called *plomero* in Argentina and Uruguay, and *gasfitero* in Peru and Ecuador (even though *gasfitero* also includes, quite logically, the idea of a gas fitter). Here we're going to list jobs as they are called in Mexico—this is a Mexican Spanish book after all, isn't it?—but you should at least know that you'll find differences with speakers from other dialects.

That said, we don't have any more options than resorting to the good old vocabulary list. Here you go!

- *El abogado, la abogada:* lawyer
- *El albañil, la albañil:* bricklayer
- *El almacenero, la almacenara, el tendero, la tendera:* storekeeper
- *El arquitecto, la arquitecta*: architect
- *El asistente, la asistente*: assistant
- *El bombero, la bombera*: firefighter
- *El cajero, la cajera*: cashier
- *El camionero, la camionera*: truck driver
- *El campesino, la campesina*: farm worker
- *El carnicero, la carnicera*: butcher
- *El carpintero, la carpintera*: carpenter
- *El cartero, la cartera*: postman
- *El casero, la casera*: landlord, landlady
- *El cazador, la cazadora*: hunter
- *El científico, la científica*: scientist
- *El cirujano, la cirujana*: surgeon
- *El cocinero, la cocinera, el chef, la chef*: cook, chef
- *El comerciante, la comerciante*: merchant
- *El conductor, la conductora, el chofer, la chofer*: driver, chauffeur
- *El consultor, la consultora*: consultant

- *El contador, la contadora, el contable, la contable*: accountant, bookkeeper
- *El dentista, la dentista*: dentist
- *El dependiente, la dependienta*: clerk
- *El electricista, la electricista*: electrician
- *El empleado, la empleada*: employee
- *El enfermero, la enfermera*: nurse
- *El escritor, la escritora*: writer
- *El farmacéutico, la farmacéutica*: pharmacist
- *El fontanero, la fontanera*: plumber
- *El gerente, la gerente*: manager
- *El granjero, la granjera*: farmer
- *El herrero, la herrera*: blacksmith
- *El ingeniero, la ingeniera*: engineer
- *El jardinero, la jardinera*: gardener
- *El juez, la jueza*: judge
- *El maestro, la maestra*: teacher
- *El marinero, la marinera, el marino, la marina*: marine
- *El mecánico, la mecánica*: mechanic
- *El médico, la médica, el doctor, la doctora*: doctor
- *El mesero, la mesera, el camarero, la camarera*: waiter, waitress
- *El obrero, la obrera*: worker
- *El padre, el cura*: priest
- *El rabino, la rabina*: rabbi

- *El panadero, la panadera*: baker
- *El peluquero, la peluquera*: hairdresser
- *El periodista, la periodista*: journalist
- *El pescador, la pescadora*: fisherman, fisherwoman
- *El pintor, la pintora*: painter
- *El policía, la policía*: policeman, policewoman
- *El portero, la portera*: doorman, doorwoman
- *El profesor, la profesora*: professor
- *El programador, la programadora*: computer programmer
- *El psicólogo, la psicóloga*: psychologist
- *El secretario, la secretaria:* secretary
- *El taxista, la taxista*: taxi driver
- *El veterinario, la veterinaria*: vet

Work-Related Vocabulary

Work vocabulary is not limited to jobs. There are also a lot of words in this semantic field—not only nouns, but also verbs and adjectives. Here you have a non-comprehensive list of work-related vocabulary:

- *La aplicación:* application
- *El aumento:* raise
- *Contratar:* to hire
- *El contrato*: contract
- *El currículum*: CV
- *Desempleado, desempleada*: unemployed

- *El desempleo*: unemployment
- *Despedir*: to fire
- *El empleado, la empleada*: employee
- *El empleador, la empleadora*: employer
- *El empleo*: employment
- *La empresa*: company
- *La entrevista de trabajo*: work interview
- *La experiencia*: experience
- *Las horas extra*: overtime
- *El jefe, la jefa*: boss
- *Jubilado, jubilada*: retired
- *Jubilarse*: to retire
- *La licencia por enfermedad/maternidad*: sick/maternity leave
- *El negocio*: business
- *La ocupación*: occupation
- *La oficina*: office
- *El oficio*: craft
- *La pasantía*: internship
- *La profesión*: profession
- *Renunciar*: to quit, to resign
- *El salario*: salary
- *El socio, la socia*: partner
- *El taller*: workshop
- *Tiempo completo*: full-time

- *Tiempo parcial*: part-time
- *La tienda*: shop
- *Tomar (un trabajo)*: to take (a job)
- *Las vacaciones pagas*: paid vacation
- *La vacante*: vacant, opening

Common Dialogues about Work

We now have a nice, lush vocabulary about careers and the work market. It's time to put it to good use. In this section, we're going to revisit some common questions and expressions that you'll surely find when speaking in Spanish.

¿A qué te dedicas?

We'll start with the most basic question: "What do you do?". There are, of course, a number of ways to ask this. You can say *¿A qué te dedicas?*, but also *¿De qué trabajas?* or *¿Cuál es tu trabajo?* ("What is your job?").

All these phrases have pretty much the same meaning. What we can't ignore is how to respond to them. There are two main ways: to use the verb *trabajar* ("to work") and to use the verb *soy* ("to be"). As in English, that depends mainly on if you have a distinguishable profession or craft or not. Let's see two examples:

- A: *¿A qué te dedicas?* (What do you do?)
  B: *Soy electricista.* (I'm an electrician)

- A: *¿Cuál es tu trabajo?* (What is your job?)

  B: *Trabajo en una fábrica de sombreros.* (I work in a hat factory)

¿Dónde trabajas?

Occupation isn't everything. You can—and probably will—ask a few other questions. A very important one refers to the place of work. It's time for *¿Dónde trabajas?* ("Where do you work?"). Let's see it in use:

- A: *¿Dónde trabajas?* (Where do you work?)

  B: *Trabajo en una oficina en el centro.* (I work in an office in the city center)

¿Para quién trabajas?

This is the famous and versatile "Who do you work for?"—you can use it with a new friend in a bar or with an enemy spy at the top of a skyscraper. In Spanish, you say *¿Para quién trabajas?* Here you have an example:

- A: *¿Para quién trabajas?* (Who do you work for?)
- B: *Trabajo para un banco.* (I work for a bank)

¿Te gusta tu trabajo?

Another fundamental question: "Do you like your job?" This is easy to ask, but hard to answer, as there are a lot of possible responses.

You can be ok, you can love it, you can hate it, or anything in between. So we'll see a few examples just to clear some options out:

- A: *¿Te gusta tu trabajo?* (Do you like your job?)
  B: *Está bien. A veces es un poco aburrido.* (It's ok. Sometimes it gets a little boring)
- A: *¿Te gusta tu trabajo?* (Do you like your job?)
  B: *¡Me encanta! Es mi trabajo soñado.* (I love it! It's my dream job)
- A: *¿Te gusta tu trabajo?* (Do you like your job?)
  B: *Lo detesto. Pero de algo hay que vivir, ¿no es cierto?* (I hate it. But you have to earn a living somehow, am I right?)

Past Tense: The Past Simple

Another stop for the grammar train! As you surely remember, a few chapters ago we talked about the present tense. In that moment, we also had to learn about verb roots, terminations and different conjugations. It was a high mountain to climb, but now we're here, and luckily we can use most of what we've learned.

You see: for regular verbs, in Spanish, the past tense affects only the ending. The root remains the same (that's how you know that it's the same verb). And you already know all that can be known about persons and pronouns. So this should be easier to absorb than the present tense. It's almost the same thing.

We still want to take things little by little, so, in this chapter, we're only going to see one kind of past: the simple past. This is used for actions that started and finished in the past. It's the difference between saying "I ate a sandwich before coming here"—meaning you ate the whole sandwich, or at least you should have—and "I was eating a sandwich when I decided to come here". In the second example, the first action was still in development when the second action took place; it was an ongoing business, not a finished one.

In Spanish, the past simple is called *pretérito perfecto simple* or *pasado perfecto simple*. As we've discussed, it follows the same rules as the present simple. You just have to change the endings. Here you have a table with the model verbs from the three conjugations:

		Amar	**Temer**	**Partir**
I	*Yo*	*am**é***	*tem**í***	*part**í***
You	*Tú (informal)*	*am**aste***	*tem**iste***	*part**iste***
	Usted (formal)	*am**ó***	*tem**ió***	*part**ió***
He/she	*Él/ella*	*am**ó***	*tem**ió***	*part**ió***
We	*Nosotros/ nosotras*	*am**amos***	*tem**imos***	*part**imos***
You	*Ustedes*	*am**aron***	*tem**ieron***	*part**ieron***
They	*Ellos/ellas*	*am**aron***	*tem**ieron***	*part**ieron***

You see? It's not that difficult. You just have to change the end of the word. The system works.

But, as you may have predicted, this doesn't end here. We have some business to take care of. We still have to talk about irregular verbs; particularly our two favorite ones, *ser* and *estar*. Luckily, that can be solved with one nice table:

		Ser	*Estar*
I	*Yo*	*fui*	*estuve*
You	*Tú (informal)*	*fuiste*	*estuviste*
	Usted (formal)	*fue*	*estuvo*
He/she	*Él/ella*	*fue*	*estuvo*
We	*Nosotros/ nosotras*	*fuimos*	*estuvimos*
You	*Ustedes*	*fueron*	*estuvieron*
They	*Ellos/ellas*	*fueron*	*estuvieron*

Key Takeaways

- In this chapter, we learned the names of a few of the most common jobs and professions.
- But work is more than just jobs: it involves a whole semantic field that includes other nouns, verbs, and adjectives.

- We review some of the most common exchanges related to work, like *¿A qué te dedicas?* ("What do you do?") or *¿Para quién trabajas?* ("Who do you work for?").
- To finish this chapter, we saw some more grammar: the past simple.

These were the main points of a very important everyday topic: work. In the next chapter, we're going to have some fun: we'll talk about Mexican idioms and typical expressions. But we still have to do some exercises on what we've just learned. Good luck with them!

Chapter Exercises

1. Fill in the blanks with the corresponding job.

    a. Trabajo en un estudio jurídico. Estudié Derecho. Soy

    _____.

    b. Trabajo en un hospital. Estudié Medicina. Soy _____.

    c. Trabajo en la cocina de un restaurante. Soy _____.

    d. Trabajo en un supermercado. Cobro a los clientes. Soy

    _____.

2. Match each job on the left with a place of work on the right.

    a. Enfermero/a   1. Comisaría

    b. Herrero/a   2. Bus

c. Conductor/a   3. Hospital

d. Policía   4. Taller

3. Fill in the blanks in the following dialogue with one of these words: *mesera, dedicas, gusta, dónde, medio tiempo, salario, bar.*

A: Entonces, Mariana, ¿a qué te _____?

B: Soy _____, ¿y tú?

A: Electricista. De acuerdo, entonces, ¿_____ trabajas?

B: En un _____ de la colonia Tabacalera. Pero no lo recomiendo.

A: ¿Qué ocurre, no te _____ trabajar allí?

B: No exactamente. El _____ es bueno, para ser un trabajo de _____. Pero ¡es muy sucio!

4. Conjugate the verbs in brackets in the past tense.

a. Helena _____ (renunciar) la semana pasada.

b. Yo _____ (contratar) a un mecánico para arreglar el coche.

c. El año pasado ustedes _____ (despedir) a la mitad de

su personal.

d. Tú _____ (tomar) ese trabajo en Jalisco, ¿no?

5. Conjugate these verbs in present simple or past simple, according to the rest of the sentence.

a. Yo _____ (ser) una persona sencilla. Solo quiero retirarme.

b. Ayer vi a Lucía en un karaoke. _____ (cantar) un bolero de Manzanero.

c. Ellos _____ (estar) en Chihuahua la semana pasada y dieron un show espectacular.

d. Ustedes no _____ (entender) mi problema, necesito la solución ahora.

6. Which of the following sentences is grammatically incorrect? Rewrite it correctly.

a. Los empleados de la empresa tienen tres semanas de vacaciones pagas, estacionamiento gratuito y un pase de gimnasio.

b. Mi dentista se retiraron, ahora tengo que buscar uno nuevo.

c. En mi oficina hay una vacante para el puesto de secretario.

d. Gabriela se dedicaba a los bienes raíces.

7. Decide whether these sentences are true or false. Correct the false ones.

a. A job can have different names across different Spanish-speaking countries.

b. Past simple is used to talk about actions that started in the past and continue up to the present.

c. A *casero* is someone who builds houses.

d. Irregular verbs become regular in the past tense.

8. Which of the following sentences is grammatically correct?

a. Los gerente no vinieron a trabajar hoy.

b. Me pasaron a buscar un taxista.

c. Quiero dejar de hacer horas extra.

d. La tienda está cerrado por el día.

9. In the next questions, choose from the words in brackets to fill in the blanks.

a. Ayer Lucrecia _____ (celebra/celebró) su cumpleaños.

b. Tú _____ (eres/estás) abogado, no te quejes.

c. Diego estudió arquitectura, es _____

(arcitecto/arquitecto).

d. ¿Ustedes _____ (conoces/conocen) a un buen

fontanero?

10. Answer these questions in your own words, in Spanish!

a. ¿A qué te dedicas?

b. ¿Dónde trabajas?

c. ¿Para quién trabajas?

d. ¿Te gusta tu trabajo?

Answer Key

1.

a. Trabajo en un estudio jurídico. Estudié Derecho. Soy

abogado/a.

b. Trabajo en un hospital. Estudié Medicina. Soy

médico(a)/doctor(a).

c. Trabajo en la cocina de un restaurante. Soy cocinero/a.

d. Trabajo en un supermercado. Cobro a los clientes. Soy cajero/a.

2.

a. Enfermero/a	3. Hospital
b. Herrero/a	4. Taller
c. Conductor/a	2. Bus
d. Policía	1. Comisaría

3.

A: Entonces, Mariana, ¿a qué te dedicas?

B: Soy mesera, ¿y tú?

A: Electricista. De acuerdo, entonces, ¿dónde trabajas?

B: En un bar de la colonia Tabacalera. Pero no lo recomiendo.

A: ¿Qué ocurre, no te gusta trabajar allí?

B: No exactamente. El salario es bueno, para ser un trabajo de medio tiempo. Pero ¡es muy sucio!

4.

a. Helena renunció la semana pasada.

b. Yo contraté a un mecánico para arreglar el coche.

c. El año pasado ustedes despidieron a la mitad de su personal.

d. Tú tomaste ese trabajo en Jalisco, ¿no?

5.

a. Yo soy una persona sencilla. Solo quiero retirarme.

b. Ayer vi a Lucía en un karaoke. Cantó un bolero de Manzanero.

c. Ellos estuvieron en Chihuahua la semana pasada y dieron un show espectacular.

d. Ustedes no entienden mi problema, necesito la solución ahora.

6.

b. Mi dentista se retiró, ahora tengo que buscar uno nuevo.

7.

a. True.

b. False. Past simple is used to talk about actions that started and finished in the past.

c. False. A *casero* is a person who rents a house.

d. False. Irregular verbs are irregular in the past tense.

8.

  c. Quiero dejar de hacer horas extra.

9.

  a. Ayer Lucrecia celebró su cumpleaños.

  b. Tú eres abogado, no te quejes.

  c. Diego estudió arquitectura, es arquitecto

  d. ¿Ustedes conocen a un buen fontanero?

Chapter 5: *¡Ándale!* Idioms and Typical Expressions of Mexico

México no se explica. En México se cree, con furia, con pasión, con desaliento.

- Carlos Fuentes

Spanish is a language spoken in many countries—you already know that, of course. This means that, inevitably, each country has its own group of expressions and words. In the previous chapter, we saw the main differences between European and Mexican Spanish, as well as some of the most common typical words in the Spanish spoken in Mexico. In this chapter, we're going to go a step further, and we are going to take a look at some of the most important idioms: those phrases that only make sense if they are said in a certain context.

So, in this chapter we are going to delve into:

- idioms and sayings in Spanish
- Mexican idioms and what they mean
- lots of dialogue examples with idioms

Are you ready? *¡Síganme los buenos!*

Idioms and Sayings in Spanish

You probably already know this, but a quick review won't hurt. An idiom is an expression that is only understood in a certain context. A saying, meanwhile, is a popular phrase that usually expresses advice or a lesson. And, above all, they are both very useful linguistic resources to sound natural when you speak in Spanish.

First, we're going to see a list of idioms and sayings that are common in all Spanish varieties; that is, you can use them interchangeably in Mexico, Costa Rica, Argentina, Spain or any other Spanish-speaking country. Let's get to them!

Dar gato por liebre

Dar gato por liebre basically means "to cheat". An equivalent idiom in English could be "to pull the wool over someone's eyes".

- *Miguel es muy ingenuo, ¡siempre le dan gato por liebre!* (Miguel is very naive, he is easily tricked!)

Haber gato encerrado

Another idiom with cats. This literally means "to have a cat locked up", but it has nothing to do with an actual cat. It is used to say that something sounds like a trap.

- *¿Marcos te dijo que no iría a la fiesta? A mí me dijo que sí iría... Aquí hay gato encerrado.* (Did Marcos tell you he wasn't going to the party? He told me he was going... There's something fishy)

Hoy por ti, mañana por mí

This idiom means, literally, "Today for you, tomorrow for me", and is used when you do someone a favor.

- *Claro que te presto el auto. Hoy por ti, mañana por mí.* (Of course I'll lend you the car. You scratch my back and I'll scratch yours)

Irse por las ramas

Literally, it means "to go through the branches". It's used to say that we are talking too much without getting to the point. We could say that its equivalent in English is "to beat around the bush".

- *Mi abuela siempre se va por las ramas cuando cuenta una de sus anécdotas* (My grandmother always talks a lot and never gets to the point when she tells one of her anecdotes)

No volar una mosca

We say that *no vuela una mosca* (literally, "not a fly flies") when there is absolute silence.

- *Durante el examen, no quiero que vuele una mosca.* (During the exam, I want you to be quiet)

Ser un caradura

Being a *caradura* means being "cheeky": being shameless or irreverent. If we look for a literal translation, we will find that *cara dura* means "hard face". This explains why a derived idiom in Spanish is *tener la cara de piedra* ("to have the face like a stone").

- *¿Me dices desagradecida a mí? Con todo lo que hago por ti. ¡Eres un caradura!* (You are calling me ungrateful? With everything I do for you. You are so cheek!)

Venir como anillo al dedo

When you receive something unexpected that you really needed, you can say *me viene como anillo al dedo*. A similar English idiom is "to be a godsend".

- *Gracias por estas gafas. Las mías se rompieron, así que me vienen como anillo al dedo.* (Thank you for these glasses. Mine broke, so they are exactly what I needed)

Mexican Idioms

We have seen a few expressions of Spanish that you can say in any Spanish-speaking region. Now, it's time to look at some Mexican idioms and sayings: expressions that are probably not understood outside the country. *¿Listo? ¡Ándale!*

A huevo

You'll probably hear this expression a lot if you go to Mexico, especially among young people. *Huevo* literally means "egg", but *a huevo* is something like "sure!". Keep in mind that this is a very colloquial expression (only say it if you are really close to the person you're talking to!).

- *¿Vamos por unas chelas?* (Do you wanna go for some beers?)
- *¡A huevo!* (Sure!)

Caer el chahuistle

When something bad has happened, Mexicans often say: *¡Ya nos cayó el chahuistle!* (something like: "We're in for it now"). The origin of this expression comes from the chahuistle, a microscopic fungus that used to affect corn crops.

- *¡Rompiste la chamarra favorita de Pedro! ¡Ya te cayó el chahuistle!* (You ripped Pedro's favorite jacket! You're in for it now!)

Echarse un coyotito

Coyotes are animals that live in Mexico, and they are nocturnal creatures. That's why *echarse un coyotito* means "to take a nap".

- *Lamento no haberte respondido antes, estaba echando un coyotito* (I'm sorry I didn't answer you before, I was taking a nap)

Hacerse pato

Although it literally means "to transform yourself into a duck", its actual meaning is "to pretend that you don't understand something", or "to pretend you haven't heard something".

- *No te hagas pato con lo que te dijo tu mamá* (Don't pretend you didn't hear what your mom told you)

No manches

No manches is used to express surprise or disbelief. It's something like English "really?", but it's a colloquial expression, so again, only use it with people you know.

- *Creo que mañana no me presentaré al examen* (I think I'll not take the exam tomorrow)
- *¡No manches! ¿Por qué? Has estado estudiando mucho* (Really? Why? You've been studying a lot)

Ponerse la de Puebla

This is a fun one, although we need to give you a little context. First of all, Puebla is a Mexican city that, like most cities, has a soccer team. The Puebla soccer team uses a shirt with a diagonal stripe from the shoulder to the waist. Secondly, the Mexican sign used to ask someone to share something is to make a diagonal movement with your hand, as if you were cutting your body in two. This is where *ponerse la (camiseta) de Puebla* comes from: it means "to share what you have".

- *Ponte la de Puebla y dame un poco de tu torta de jamón* (Come on, be good and share some of your ham sandwich with me)

Creerse muy muy

Te crees muy muy literally means: "You think you're very-very". I know, it doesn't seem to make sense, but it's used to tell a person that they're very vain. It's also used to tell someone that they think they are very brave, but they brag too much about their deeds. Maybe a good equivalent in English is "to think oneself is such a big deal".

- *Sandra siempre está alardeando. Se cree muy muy.* (Sandra is always bragging. She thinks she's such a big deal)

Other Mexican Idioms and Sayings

Let's take a look at a few more Mexican idiomatic expressions and their meanings.

Mexican Idiom	Meaning
Aguanta vara	Keep your promises or be brave
A darle que es mole de olla	Let's do it fast, because there's

	no time
Dar el avión	To ignore
De chile, mole y pozole	Of all varieties
Hacer el paro	To do a favor
Nel	No
¿Neta?	Really?
Ponerle mucha crema a los tacos	To be too dramatic
¡Qué padre!	So cool!
Tirar barra	To do nothing, to be lazy
Ya salió el peine	The truth about something came out

Key Takeaways

- Saying and idioms are important to understand real Spanish, the one spoken by actual people. Also, they are a good way to sound more natural.
- There are some sayings and idioms in Spanish that you can use in any Spanish-speaking country. A few examples are:
  - *Ser un caradura.*
  - *Haber gato encerrado.*
  - *No volar una mosca .*

- Other expressions are only common in Mexican Spanish, such as:
    - *A huevo.*
    - *No manches.*
    - *Te crees muy muy.*

In chapter 6, we're going to learn all about a very important aspect of everyday life: shopping. But first, how about a few exercises to put everything you've learned into practice?

Chapter Exercises

1. Match each idiom on the left with its meaning on the right.

    a. No te hagas pato   1. I'll take a nap

    b. Ponte la de Puebla with me   2. Share a piece

    c. Me voy a echar un coyotito you didn't hear   3. Don't pretend

    d. Ya nos cayó el chahuistle now   4. We're in trouble

2. Can you identify all the idioms in the following story?

Hoy fue mi primer día de clases en la universidad. Estaba nerviosa y anoche casi no pegué ojo, pero fue un día muy bonito. Hice buenas migas con una chica llamada Fernanda. Habla hasta por los codos, pero es muy simpática. También conocí a un chico llamado Roberto que se cree muy muy.

Al mediodía, Fernanda y yo salimos a almorzar. Yo ordené un plato de pastas (se me hizo agua la boca cuando el camarero llegó con la orden). Fernanda pidió pizza con piña. A mí no me gusta, pero sobre gustos no hay nada escrito. El almuerzo nos costó un ojo de la cara. Ya sabemos que no tenemos que volver a ese restaurante. De todas formas, la pasta estaba buenísima. Después de todo, ¡quien no arriesga, no gana!

3. Below there is a list of the meanings of all the idioms from the previous story. Follow the example and write the idiom in Spanish next to it.

   a. To get along → Hacer buenas migas
   b. To think oneself to be a big deal
   c. Don't sleep
   d. Something's very expensive
   e. Tastes are a personal thing
   f. Taking risks can pay off
   g. Feel like eating something
   h. To talk too much

4. Now, how about we check your reading comprehension?

   a. What does the protagonist think about Fernanda and about Roberto?
   b. What did the protagonist order for lunch and what did Fernanda order?

c. Why doesn't the protagonist want to go back to the restaurant?

d. Why was the protagonist nervous the night before?

5. Following the example, complete the following sentences with the correct idioms. You'll have to conjugate the verbs in the present simple.

a. Carlos me dijo que estaba en su casa, pero lo llamé y nadie respondió. Aquí *hay gato encerrado* (haber gato encerrado).

b. Miguel siempre _____ (ponerse la de Puebla) y nos invita a todos a una ronda de chelas.

c. Mi madre siempre _____ (echarse un coyotito) los domingos por la tarde.

d. Mis alumnos _____ (hablar hasta por los codos).

6. Match each idiom on the left with its meaning on the right.

a. Dar el avión	1. To do a favor
b. Hacer el paro	2. To be too dramatic
c. Tirar barra	3. To ignore
d. Ponerle mucha crema a los tacos	4. To do nothing

7. The following dialogue has a few idioms, but they have mistakes. Can you correct them?

A: ¿Te gusta mi nuevo carro, Luis?

B: ¡Qué madre! ¿Cuándo te lo compraste?

A: El mes pasado. Estaba indeciso entre un montón de carros distintos. Había de chile, maíz y pozole. Pero al final me decidí por este.

B: Me imagino que te habrá costado una ceja de la cara.

A: ¡Mel! Estaba de oferta.

8. Choose which idiom you would use in each of the following situations.

- Situation 1: The waiter arrives with your dish and you can't wait to eat it.

   a) Aquí hay gato encerrado

   b) Se me hace agua la boca

   c) Esto es pan comido

- Situation 2: A person talks about all the money they have.

   a) Ponte la de Puebla

   b) No te hagas pato

   c) Te crees muy muy

- Situation 3: Your best friend invites you to a party.

   a) ¡A huevo!

   b) ¡No manches!

   c) ¡Qué padre!

9. Put the following dialogue in order.

   1. A huevo, me parece una idea padre. Pero estoy un poco cansada ahora.

2. ¿Qué te parece si vamos por unas chelas a un antro?

3. Neta. Tiremos barra un rato y después vamos.

4. ¿Por qué no te echas un coyotito antes?

10. Fill in the blanks.

Idiom	Literal translation	Meaning
Agarra la vara	Take the stick	Keep your promises
Dar el avión	To give the airplane	
	To put a lot of cream on the tacos	To be too dramatic
Irse por las ramas		

Answer Key

1.

    a. No te hagas pato 3. Don't pretend you didn't hear

    b. Ponte la de Puebla 2. Share a piece with me

    c. Me voy a echar un coyotito 1. I'll take a nap

    d. Ya nos cayó el chahuistle 4. We're in trouble now

2.

no pegar ojo, hacer buenas migas, hablar hasta por los codos, creerse muy muy, hacerse agua la boca, sobre gustos no hay nada escrito, costar un ojo de la cara, quien no arriesga no gana.

3.

a. To get along → Hacer buenas migas

b. To think oneself to be a big deal → Creerse muy muy

c. Don't sleep → No pegar ojo

d. Something's very expensive → Costar un ojo de la cara

e. Tastes are a personal thing → Sobre gustos no hay nada escrito

f. To take risks can pay off → Quien no arriesga, no gana

g. Feel like eating something → Hacerse agua la boca

h. To talk too much → Hablar hasta por los codos

4.

a. The protagonist thinks that Fernanda talks a lot and that Roberto is vain.

b. The protagonist ordered a plate of pasta. Fernanda ordered pizza with pineapple.

c. Because it is very expensive.

d. Because today was her first day of class at the university.

5.

a. hay gato encerrado

b. se pone la de Puebla

c. se echa un coyotito

d. hablan hasta por los codos

6.

a. Dar el avión 3. To ignore

b. Hacer el paro 1. To do a favor

c. Tirar barra 4. To do nothing

d. Ponerle mucha crema a los tacos 2. To be too dramatic

7.

A: ¿Te gusta mi nuevo carro, Luis?

B: ¡Qué padre! ¿Cuándo te lo compraste?

A: El mes pasado. Estaba indeciso entre un montón de carros distintos. Había de chile, mole y pozole. Pero al final me decidí por este.

B: Me imagino que te habrá costado un ojo de la cara.

A: ¡Nel! Estaba de oferta.

8.

- Situation 1: b) Se me hace agua la boca

- Situation 2: c) Te crees muy muy

- Situation 3: a) ¡A huevo!

9.

¿Qué te parece si vamos por unas chelas a un antro?

A huevo, me parece una idea padre. Pero estoy un poco cansada ahora.

¿Por qué no te echas un coyotito antes?

Neta. Tiremos barra un rato y después vamos.

10.

Idiom	Literal translation	Meaning
Agarra la vara	Take the stick	Keep your promises

Dar el avión	To give the airplane	To ignore
Ponerle mucha crema a los tacos	To put a lot of cream on the tacos	To be too dramatic
Irse por las ramas	To go through the branches	To beat around the bush

Wait! Let's Have a Middle-Book Quiz

Well, you've made it this far: we're now halfway through the book. Let's have a round of applause, everybody! We know it wasn't easy; you had to fight against grammar and vocabulary, so you really deserve recognition.

After our little celebration, it's time to make a quick recap. Stop and take a breath. Until now, we've seen a lot of very complicated concepts, from verbal conjugations to noun-adjective agreement. We got acquainted with some Mexican idioms and expressions, and we learned the richness of their vocabulary. That is a lot to take in.

So we figured that, at this stage, you may need to go over some of what you've learned. After all, exercising is a healthy habit—or that's what people say. This recap will assure you a strong foundation, upon which we're going to keep building until the end of the book. So, in this middle-book quiz, we're going to go over:

- greetings, questions and introductions
- present and past tenses

- different pronouns and conjugations: *tú, usted, ustedes, vosotros/vosotras*
- idioms, sayings and a lot more vocabulary

It sounds doable, doesn't it? We thought so. Let's begin!

1. In the next sentences, choose from the words in brackets to fill in the blanks.

   a. Ayer Sofía _____ (llega/llegó) tarde a chambear.

   b. ¿Usted _____ (sabe/sabes) dónde queda la estación de bus?

   c. _____ (disculpe/disculpa), ¿cuál es su nombre?

   d. Rodrigo _____ (está/es) listo para salir.

2. Complete these questions with the corresponding interrogative pronoun or adverb.

   a. ¿_____ te llamas?

   b. ¿_____ está la estación?

   c. ¿_____ es tu trabajo?

   d. ¿Para _____ trabajas?

3. Match each wh-word on the left with its Spanish translation on the right.

   a. Who   1. Por qué

   b. What   2. Cuándo

   c. When   3. Dónde

d. Where   4. Qué

e. Why   5. Quién

4. Decide whether the following statements are true or false. Correct the false ones.

    a. *Tú* is the formal pronoun of the second person singular, and *usted* is the informal pronoun.

    b. In the infinitive, Spanish verbs have three possible endings: AR, ER and IR.

    c. *¿Cómo estás?* and *¿Qué tal?* are ways of saying goodbye.

    d. The two most important irregular verbs in Spanish are *ser* and *estar*.

5. Read the following dialogue and identify all the words and expressions of Mexican slang.

A: ¿Qué harás esta noche, Pedro?

B: María me invitó a una fiesta en un antro.

A: ¡Suena padrísimo!

B: Sí, pero estoy con poca lana. Además, no conozco a nadie.

Oye, Juan, ¿por qué no vienes con nosotros?

A: Me gustaría, pero no puedo.

B: No manches, ¿por qué?

A: Mañana tengo que chambear temprano.

B: Vamos, Juan, hazme el paro. Solo platicaremos un rato y beberemos unas chelas.

A: A huevo, está bien. ¡Pero solo un ratito!

6. Now, answer (in Spanish!) the following questions about the dialogue.

   a. ¿Por qué Pedro no quiere ir a la fiesta en el antro?

   b. ¿Por qué Juan no puede acompañarlo?

   c. ¿Cómo convence Pedro a Juan para que vaya con él a la fiesta?

   d. ¿Por cuánto tiempo irá Juan a la fiesta?

7. Match each question on the left with its answer on the right.

   a. ¿Cuál es tu nombre?   1. Un compositor de boleros.

   b. ¿Dónde estuviste ayer?   2.   ¡Claro!

   c. ¿Quieres ir al parque mañana?   3.   Juliana.

   d. ¿Quién fue Armando Manzanero?   4.   En   Jalisco.

8. The following sentences are grammatically incorrect. Can you correct them?

   a. Me encantan regar las plantas por la mañana.

b. Tengo dos hijas; la una vive en Ciudad de México, la otra en Guadalajara.

c. Mañana tengo una reunión a la once de la mañana.

d. Mi comida favorito son los tamales.

9. Fill in the blanks in the following sentences with one of these words: *maestra, banco, mesero, veterinaria.*

a. Marcelo estudió _____.

b. Dolores es _____ porque estudió magisterio.

c. Ulises trabaja como _____ en un bar.

d. Tomás es gerente en el _____.

10. Conjugate the verbs in brackets in the past simple.
a. Me _____ (gustar) ir a Playa del Carmen el verano pasado.
b. Mi casamiento _____ (ser) el mes pasado.
c. Gerardo y Romina _____ (tener) mellizos.
d. El juguete favorito de mi hijo se _____ (romper).

11. Read this news article.
Encuentran fósil de dinosaurio en Coahuila

Investigadores del Instituto de Antropología e Historia de

México anunciaron el hallazgo del *Tlatolophus galorum*, un

inmenso dinosaurio herbívoro, cerca de General Cepeda, al norte del país. Los paleontólogos a cargo revelaron que rescataron casi el 80% del cráneo del animal y más de 30 fragmentos óseos.

"Se trata de un descubrimiento importante", dice Ángel Ramírez Velasco, director de la operación. "Los parasaurolophus, el tipo de dinosaurios al que este *tlatolophus* pertenece, solo se habían encontrado en los Estados Unidos y Canadá. El *galorum* es una especie nueva dentro de ese grupo, la más austral de todas".

El *Tlatolophus galorum* vivió en Norteamérica hace más de setenta millones de años, durante el período Cretácico. Era un herbívoro de gran tamaño, que podía alcanzar los ocho metros de largo. Se distinguía por la inmensa cresta de más de un metro que llevaba en su cráneo.

La palabra *tlatolophus* tiene un origen doble. Por un lado, el término *lophus* significa "cresta" en griego, cosa que señala su rasgo más característico. Por el otro, *tlatolli* viene del náhuatl, y significa "palabra". Esto se debe a que los parasaurolophus, como otros dinosaurios, tenían una serie inusual de pasajes entre la nariz y la tráquea. Eso hace suponer que podían emitir sonidos con función comunicativa. Así es: el nuevo dinosaurio mexicano ¡era un dinosaurio parlante!

12. After reading the article, answer the following questions.

a. Near which city was the dinosaur found?

b. Who was in charge of the team that found it?

c. What's the Spanish name for the people whose job is to look for dinosaurs?

d. What does *tlatolli* mean?

13. Conjugate the verbs in brackets in the present simple.

a. _____ (estar) muy contento por tu nuevo trabajo.

b. María _____ (ser) una persona muy simpática.

c. Lucas _____ (tener) una casa muy bonita.

d. Mis padres _____ (viajar) muy seguido a Ciudad de México.

14. *Ándale, córrele* or *muévanle*? In each sentence decide which one is the correct option.

a. ¡_____, Miguel, o llegaremos tarde a la universidad!

b. ¡Levántate, _____!

c. _____, chicos, tenemos que irnos.

15. The following table shows the simple past tense of the verb *cocinar* ("to cook"), but it is incomplete. Can you fill in the blanks?

		Cocinar
I	*Yo*	*cociné*
You	*Tú (informal)*	
	Usted (formal)	*cocinó*
He/she		
We		*cocinamos*
	Ustedes	
They	*Ellos/ellas*	*cocinaron*

Answer Key

1.

    a. Ayer Sofía llegó tarde a chambear.

    b. ¿Usted sabe dónde queda la estación de bus?

    c. Disculpe, ¿cuál es su nombre?

    d. Rodrigo está listo para salir.

2.

    a. ¿Cómo te llamas?

    b. ¿Dónde está la estación?

    c. ¿Cómo es tu trabajo?

    d. ¿Para quién trabajas?

3.

    a. Who 5. Quién

    b. What 4. Qué

    c. When 2. Cuándo

    d. Where 3. Dónde

    e. Why 1. Por qué

4.

    a. False. *Tú* is informal, and *usted* is formal.

    b. True.

    c. False. They're ways of saying hello.

    d. True.

5. antro, padrísimo, lana, no manches, chambear, hazme el paro, platicamos, chelas, a huevo.

6.

   a. Porque tiene poca lana y no conoce a nadie.

   b. Porque mañana tiene que chambear temprano.

   c. Le dice que solo platicarán un poco y beberán unas chelas.

   d. Por un ratito.

7.

   a. ¿Cuál es tu nombre? 3. Juliana.

   b. ¿Dónde estuviste ayer? 4. En Jalisco.

   c. ¿Quiéres ir al parque mañana? 2. ¡Claro!

   d. ¿Quién es Armando Manzanero? 1. Un compositor de boleros.

8.

   a. Me encanta regar las plantas por la mañana.

   b. Tengo dos hijas; una vive en Ciudad de México, la otra en Guadalajara.

   c. Mañana tengo una reunión a las once de la mañana.

   d. Mi comida favorita son los tamales.

9.

   a. Marcelo estudió veterinaria.

   b. Dolores es maestra porque estudió magisterio

   c. Ulises trabaja como mesero en un bar.

   d. Tomás es gerente en el banco.

10.

   a. Me gustó ir a Playa del Carmen el verano pasado.

   b. Mi casamiento fue el mes pasado.

c. Gerardo y Romina tuvieron mellizos.

d. El juguete favorito de mi hijo se rompió.

11.

a. General Cepeda

b. Ángel Ramírez Velasco

c. Paleontólogos

d. Palabra

12.

a. Estoy muy contento por tu nuevo trabajo.

b. María es una persona muy simpática.

c. Lucas tiene una casa muy bonita.

d. Mis padres viajan muy seguido a Ciudad de México.

13.

a. ¡Córrele, Miguel, o llegaremos tarde a la universidad!

b. ¡Levántate, ándale!

c. Muévanle, chicos, tenemos que irnos.

14.

		Cocinar
I	*Yo*	*cociné*
You	*Tú (informal)*	cocinaste
	Usted (formal)	cocinó

He/she	Él/ella	cocinó
We	Nosotros/nosotras	cocinamos
You	Ustedes	cocinaron
They	Ellos/ellas	cocinaron

Chapter 6: *¿Vamos de compras?* All about Shopping

Quien a vender va al mercado, si lleva de todo vende algo.

- Mexican proverb

"How much is that shirt?", "Do you take credit card?", "Thanks, I'm just looking". Undoubtedly, those phrases are part of the essential phrase book of anyone who likes to go shopping. But how do you say them in Spanish? And, especially, how do you say them in Mexican Spanish? In this chapter we will dive into:

- *pretérito imperfecto*
- shopping-related vocabulary
- useful phrases for shopping
- places to go shopping in Mexico
- Mexican Spanish words for clothes

Are you ready? *¡Vamos de compras!*

Pretérito Imperfecto

First of all, let's see a bit of grammar. It's time to immerse ourselves in the *pretérito imperfecto*, a verb tense in Spanish used to talk about an action that happened in the past, but which we don't know exactly when it took place. For example, we can use this tense to talk about things that we used to do before, or things that used to be a certain way.

To conjugate the *pretérito imperfecto* with regular verbs, you need to remove the endings of the verbs in the infinitive (AR, ER or IR) and add the corresponding endings, as detailed in the table below:

	Verbs ending in AR	Verbs ending in ER and IR
Yo	-aba	-ía
Tú	-abas	-ías
Él/ella	-aba	-ía
Nosotros/nosotras	-ábamos	-íamos
Ustedes	-aban	-ían
Ellos/ellas	-aban	-ían

The rules of the table apply to all verbs except irregular ones, which tend to follow their own capricious rules. The good news is that, in Spanish, there are only three verbs that are irregular in the *pretérito imperfecto*: *ser* ("to be"), *ir* ("to go") and *ver* ("to see"). Let's see how to conjugate them.

	Ser	Ir	Ver

Yo	era	iba	veía
Tú	eras	ibas	veías
Él/ella	era	iba	veía
Nosotros/ nosotras	éramos	íbamos	veíamos
Ustedes	eran	iban	veían
Ellos/ellas	eran	iban	veían

Now, let's see in more detail (and with example sentences) in which situations we should use the *pretérito imperfecto*. We use it:

1. To talk about habitual actions in the past.
- *Cuando **era** pequeño, siempre **venía** de vacaciones a Cancún.* (When I was little, I always came to Cancun on holidays)
2. To talk about the state of something or someone in the past.
- *Esta tienda **estaba** llena de gente la última vez que vine.* (This store was full of people the last time I came)
3. To talk about an action that is interrupted by another.
- ***Caminaba** por la calle cuando encontré a Marcos, un viejo amigo.* (I was walking down the street when I ran into Marcos, an old friend)

Shopping-Related Vocabulary

Grammar section is over! (We know it: it can be a bit boring sometimes, but we need it if we want to learn a new language.) Now, it's time for you to learn how to express yourself properly when shopping in Mexico.

First, we need to know that the Spanish verb for "to buy" is *comprar,* and "to sell" is *vender.* Let's explore a list with more shopping-related vocabulary:

Spanish	English
el aparador	storefront
barato, barata	cheap
buen precio	good price
la caja	cash register
el cajero, la cajera	cashier
el cambio	change
caro, cara	expensive
el centro comercial	mall
el comercio	commerce
el cliente, la clienta	client
el dependiente, la dependienta	clerk

el descuento	discount
la devolución	return
el dinero	money
el efectivo	cash
la lana	money (colloquial)
la marca	brand
la oferta	sale
el precio	price
el probador	fitting room
probarse	to try on
la promoción	promotion
regatear	to bargain
la talla	size
la tienda	store

Useful Phrases for Shopping

This is a list of phrases that you may find useful when you are shopping in Mexico.

- *¿Tiene una talla más grande?* (Do you have a bigger size?)
- *¿Tiene una talla más pequeña?* (Do you have a smaller size?)

- *¿Puedo pagar con tarjeta de crédito?* (Can I pay with credit card?)
- *¿Acepta tarjeta?* (Do you take credit card?)
- *Solo estoy mirando, gracias* (I'm just looking, thanks)
- *Disculpe, ¿me puede ayudar?* (Excuse me, can you help me?)
- *¿Me lo puedo probar?* (Can I try it on?)
- *¿Dónde están los probadores?* (Where are the fitting rooms?)
- *¿Tiene cambio o devolución?* (Can I exchange it or return it?)

Now, let's see the phrases that an employee in a store might say to you.

- *¿Qué busca? / ¿Qué está buscando?* (What are you looking for?)
- *¿Lo/la puedo ayudar?* (Can I help you?)
- *Si me necesita, estoy por aquí* (If you need me, I'm over here)
- *¿Qué talla necesita?* (What size do you need?)
- *¿Necesita una talla más/menos?* (Do you need a bigger/smaller size?)
- *¿Cómo le quedó?* (How did it go?)
- *Solo aceptamos efectivo.* (We only take cash)
- *¿Desea ver alguna otra cosa?* (Is there anything else you want to see?)

To inquire about the price of something, there are a few questions you can ask. They all mean essentially the same thing: "How much is it?"

- *¿Cuánto sale? / ¿Cuánto cuesta? / ¿Cuánto vale?*
- *¿Qué sale? / ¿Qué cuesta? / ¿Qué vale?*
- *¿A cuánto los...?*
- *¿Qué precio tiene?*

Haggling isn't common in city stores. Actually, trying to negotiate a price in a store could be seen as rude. However, this practice is common in second-hand markets and some street shops. Some of the most typical questions when bargaining are:

- *¿Cuánto pide por...?* (How much for...?)
- *Le doy...* (I'll give you...)
- *Tengo...* (I have...)
- *¿En cuánto me deja...?* (What will you take for...?)

Places To Go Shopping in Mexico

Of course, there are plenty of places you could go shopping. Let's see some of them.

Centro comercial. Shopping malls are called *centros comerciales*, although it's also common to call them simply "malls". Malls typically have:

- *Muchos pisos* (multiple floors)
- *Un estacionamiento* (a parking lot)
- *Muchas tiendas* (many stores)
- *Una plaza de comidas* (a food court)
- *Una zona de juegos para niños* (a children's play area)

Centro de la ciudad. Normally, cities and towns have their downtown area. This area is known as *centro de la ciudad* or just *centro*, and usually has a lot of shops. In big cities, the downtown is generally well-connected to other districts by many bus or subway lines.

Mercados callejeros. The *mercados callejeros* ("street markets" or "flea markets") are normally set up in the open air, and have stalls that sell different things, from food to clothes or antiques (*antigüedades* in Spanish).

Tiendas. Let's see a list of stores that you may need to visit at some point if you go to Mexico.

Spanish	English
el banco	bank
la barbería	barbershop
la cafetería	coffee store
la carnicería	butcher shop

Spanish	English
la farmacia	pharmacy
la ferretería	hardware store
la gasolinera	gas station
el hipermercado	hypermarket
la lavandería	laundry
la librería	bookshop
el mercado	market
el minisúper	convenience store
la panadería	bakery
la pastelería	cake shop
la peluquería	hairdressing
la pescadería	fish shop
el supermercado	supermarket
la tienda de abarrotes	grocery store

Mexican Spanish Words for Clothes

Now, imagine that you are in a clothing store and you want to buy something. It's important that you know how to say clothes in Mexican Spanish!

Spanish	English

el bolso	bag
el brasier	bra
la bufanda	scarf
los calcetines	socks
la chamarra	jacket
la falda	skirt
los guantes	gloves
las pantaletas	panties
los pantalones de mezclilla	jeans
la playera	shirt
el sombrero	hat
la sudadera	hoodie
el suéter	sweater
los tenis	sneakers
el traje de baño	swimsuit
la trusa	underpants
el vestido	dress
los zapatos	shoes

Key Takeaways

- The *pretérito imperfecto* is used to talk about an indeterminate past. To conjugate regular verbs in this tense, you just need to remove the ending of the infinitive (AR, ER or IR) and add the corresponding ending.
- There are only three irregular verbs in the *pretérito imperfecto*: *ser*, *ir* and *ver*.
- Within the shopping-related vocabulary, we find important words as *barato* ("cheap"), *caro* ("expensive") or *oferta* ("sale").
- Haggling is not common in city stores, although it is expected in street markets.
- There are many places you could go shopping in Mexico, such as *centros comerciales* ("shopping malls"), *el centro de la ciudad* ("downtown"), *mercados callejeros* ("street markets") and *tiendas* ("stores").

As we have made clear in this chapter, knowing how to buy is very important. Now that's clear, the next step is to know how to handle yourself properly when traveling. Let's see it in the next chapter! But before, we leave you with some exercises so that you can practice everything you have learned.

Chapter Exercises

1. Fill in the blanks in the following table to form the *pretérito imperfecto* of the verbs *comprar* ("to buy") and *vender* ("to sell").

	Comprar	Vender
Yo	compraba	vendía
Tú		
Él/ella		
Nosotros/nosotras		
Ustedes		
Ellos/ellas		

2. Conjugate the verbs in brackets in *pretérito imperfecto* to complete the following text. Cuando _____ (ser) niña, me _____ (encantar) caminar por el centro de Guadalajara. ¡Recuerdo que _____ (mirar) los aparadores de las tiendas de muñecas y _____ (querer) comprarme todas!

3. How much vocabulary do you remember? Match each Spanish word on the left with its English translation on the right.

    a. aparador   1. cash

b. dependiente   2. storefront

c. regatear   3. bargain

d. efectivo   4. clerk

4. The following sentences are grammatically incorrect. Can you correct them?

    a. ¿Tiene un talla más grande?

    b. Estoy busco un pantalón de mezclilla.

    c. ¿Cuánto cuestan el pan?

    d. ¿Me lo puedo probarlo?

5. Fill in the blanks in this dialogue with one of these words: *traje de baño, pantalones de mezclilla, centro comercial, comprar, playera, tarjeta de crédito.*
A: ¿Me acompañas a _____ algo de ropa? Necesito unos _____ nuevos y una _____.
B: Claro. Yo tengo que comprarme un nuevo _____, porque se acerca el verano. ¿Dónde quieres ir?
A: Conozco un bonito _____ por aquí.
B: De acuerdo, vamos. No olvides llevar tu _____.

6. Where would you say each of the following phrases?

    a. ¿Tiene una talla más grande?   1. Ferretería

b. Estoy buscando un destornillador   2. Tienda de ropa

c. ¿Tiene analgésicos?   3.   Feria callejera

d. ¿En cuánto me lo deja?   4. Farmacia

7. In the next sentences, choose from the words in brackets to fill in the blanks.

a. En esa tienda, no aceptan _____ (carta/tarjeta) de crédito.

b. El centro comercial tiene una _____ (plaza de comidas/plaza de alimentos).

c. Ese pantalón es muy _____ (caro/expensivo).

d. El _____ (tienda/minisúper) está abierto hasta tarde.

8. Write a possible question for each of the following answers.
a. Question: _____
Answer: Por supuesto que se lo puede probar.

b.   Question: _____
Answer: Cincuenta pesos.

c.   Question: _____

Answer: Sí, aceptamos tarjeta de crédito.

9. Fill in the blanks with the corresponding store.

   a. En la _____ venden mariscos.

   b. En la _____ venden pasteles.

   c. En la _____ venden medicamentos.

   d. En la _____ venden carne.

10. Put the following items of clothing under the corresponding category: *guantes, playera, tenis, pantalones de mezclilla, sombrero.*

Cabeza	Manos	Torso	Piernas	Pies

Answer Key

1.

	Comprar	Vender
Yo	compraba	vendía
Tú	comprabas	vendías
Él/ella	compraba	vendía
Nosotros/nosotras	comprábamos	vendíamos
Ustedes	compraban	vendían
Ellos/ellas	compraban	vendían

2. Cuando era niña, me encantaba caminar por el centro de Guadalajara. ¡Recuerdo que miraba los aparadores de las tiendas de muñecas y quería comprarme todas!

3.

a. aparador 2. storefront

b. dependiente 4. clerk

c. regatear 3. bargain

d. efectivo 1. cash

4.

a. ¿Tienes una talla más grande?

b. Estoy buscando un pantalón de mezclilla.

c. ¿Cuánto cuesta el pan?

d. ¿Me lo puedo probar?

5.

A: ¿Me acompañas a comprar algo de ropa? Necesito unos pantalones de mezclilla nuevos y una playera.

B: Claro. Yo tengo que comprarme un nuevo traje de baño, porque se acerca el verano. ¿Dónde quieres ir?

A: Conozco un bonito centro comercial por aquí.

B: De acuerdo, vamos. No olvides llevar tu tarjeta de crédito.

6.

a. ¿Tiene una talla más grande? 2. Tienda de ropa

b. Estoy buscando un destornillador 1. Ferretería

c. ¿Tiene analgésicos? 4. Farmacia

d. ¿En cuánto me lo deja? 3. Feria callejera

7.

a. En esa tienda, no aceptan tarjeta de crédito.

b. El centro comercial tiene una plaza de comidas.

c. Ese pantalón es muy caro.

d. El minisúper está abierto hasta tarde.

8.

a. ¿Me lo puedo probar?

b. ¿Cuánto cuesta?

c. ¿Aceptan tarjeta de crédito?

9.

a. En la pescadería venden mariscos.

b. En la pastelería venden pasteles.

c. En la farmacia venden medicamentos.

d. En la carnicería venden carne.

10.

Cabeza	Manos	Torso	Piernas	Pies
sombrero	guantes	playera	pantalones de mezclillas	tenis

Chapter 7: Traveling, Coming and Going

El deseo del viaje es innato en los hombres; no es enteramente humano aquel que no lo haya sentido alguna vez.

- Octavio Paz

Imagine you're finally traveling to Mexico. You have everything ready: your suitcase, your passport, the hotel reservations... There's only one thing missing: the correct vocabulary! In this chapter, we will see all the necessary words, phrases and ways to ask for directions you will undoubtedly need for a trip to Mexico. We're going to see:

- phrases and words needed in an airport
- how to ask for directions in Mexico
- prepositions and adverbs of place
- places in Mexico
- traveling vocabulary

¿Estás listo? ¡Vamos!

Don't Miss Your Flight!

Airports can be stressful places. It makes sense, considering that we're generally in a race against the clock when we're there. Planes unfortunately won't wait for us if we're delayed, and no one wants to miss a flight!

Therefore, it's important that you know how to handle yourself in an airport. This vocabulary will be useful if you are traveling to Mexico, as well as to any other Spanish-speaking country.

The first thing we have to do is familiarize ourselves with the word *equipaje*, which in English means "baggage" or just "bags". This is the set of elements you carry with you during a trip. Let's see an example sentence:

- *Tengo que empacar mi equipaje para el viaje a Cancún.* (I have to pack my bags for the trip to Cancun)

Then we have the specific items we take with us. In Mexican Spanish, "suitcase" is *maleta. Las maletas* are the ones that you check at a counter before getting on the plane (this action is known as *despachar*), while the things you carry with you are known as *el bolso de mano* or *el equipaje de mano*. The carry-on bag is called *la maleta de mano*, although you can also use the term in English: *la maleta carry-on*. Sometimes, people carry *una mochila* ("backpack") or only *una riñonera* ("fanny pack") with them.

Let's see a few examples.

- *Señor, tiene que despachar esa maleta, aunque puede llevar la mochila como equipaje de mano.* (Sir, you have to check that suitcase, although you can take the backpack as a handbag)
- *Su maleta de mano es demasiado grande para viajar en la cabina del avión, así que tendrá que despacharla.* (Your carry-on bag is too big to travel in the cabin of the plane, so you'll have to check it)
- *Disculpe, ¿dónde se encuentra el mostrador de la aerolínea para despachar mis maletas?* (Excuse me, where is the airline counter to check my bags?)

If you have ever traveled by plane, you surely know that airlines are usually quite strict about the weight of your luggage. As a general rule, each passenger can check a bag of up to 50 pounds in economy class. Keep in mind that, in all Spanish-speaking countries, the weight measure used is the kilogram (kg). In Mexico, most airlines allow up to 20 or 22 kg per checked bag, while the weight of the carry-on bag has to be between 7 and 10 kg (approximately between 15 and 20 pounds).

We have learned a few words and verbs that will help you get around in an airport. But there are many more! Let's see a list of airport vocabulary:

Spanish	English
abordar	to board
la aduana	customs
la aerolínea	airline
el aeromozo, la aeromoza	flight attendant
el aeropuerto	airport
aterrizar	to land
el avión	airplane
el azafato, la azafata	flight attendant or stewardess
la bodega del avión	aircraft hold
el boleto	ticket
el bolso de mano	handbag
el chaleco salvavidas	lifejacket
el cinturón de seguridad	seat belt
la clase turista	economy class
despegar	to take off
el equipaje	baggage
la escala	layover
llegadas	arrivals
el pasajero	passenger

la primera clase	first class
la puerta de embarque	boarding gate
la reserva	booking
libre de impuestos	duty free
migraciones	immigration office
el mostrador de facturación	check-in desk
salidas	departures
la tarjeta de embarque	boarding pass
la tripulación	crew
el vuelo (a tiempo/retrasado/cancelado)	flight (on time/delayed/canceled)

How to Ask for Directions in the Streets of Mexico

¡Felicidades! You flew to Mexico and now you're about to leave the hotel for the first time to walk around the city. That means it's time for you to learn a few useful phrases for your trip.

Remember that, as we saw in the first chapter of the book, you should use polite words like *disculpe* or *perdone* at the beginning of the phrases. And don't forget about *por favor* and *gracias* (especially when dealing with people you don't know). You can also add polite constructions, like *¿Me podría indicar…?* ("Could you tell me…?") or *¿Me diría…?* ("Would you tell me…?").

Let's take a look at the most common questions to ask for directions. There are also some example sentences for you to see them in use.

- **¿Dónde está...?**
  - *Disculpe, ¿dónde está la parada del autobús?* (Excuse me, where is the bus stop?)
- **¿Dónde hay...?**
  - *Perdone, ¿dónde hay una casa de cambio por aquí?* (Excuse me, where can I find a currency exchange around here?)
- **¿Dónde queda...?**
  - *¿Dónde queda el centro de la ciudad?* (Where is the city center?)
- **¿Dónde es...?**
  - *Disculpe, ¿me puede indicar dónde es la plaza principal?* (Excuse me, can you tell me where the main square is?)
- **¿Cómo llego a...?**
  - *¿Me diría cómo llego al aeropuerto, por favor?* (Could you tell me how to get to the airport, please?)
- **¿Cómo puedo ir a...?**
  - *Perdone, ¿cómo puedo ir a la zona de restaurantes?* (Excuse me, how can I get to the food court?)
- **¿Cómo puedo llegar a...?**

○ *¿Cómo puedo llegar a un cajero automático?* (How can I get to an ATM?)

Prepositions and Adverbs of Place

These types of words are extremely necessary to ask and give directions, and also to understand when someone gives directions to us. Let's see some of them:

Preposition / Adverb	Translation	Example
en	in, inside of, on top of	*Mi casa está <u>en</u> la colonia Roma.*
encima de	on top of	*<u>Encima</u> de la montaña está el teleférico.*
dentro de	inside of	*La oficina de información está <u>dentro</u> de ese edificio.*
fuera de	outside of	*No está permitido trasladar los objetos <u>fuera del</u> hotel.*
delante de	in front of	*<u>Delante de</u> esa tienda hay un cajero automático.*
detrás de	behind	*<u>Detrás</u> del hotel hay una playa.*

al lado de	beside	*La estación del metro está <u>al lado de</u> ese museo.*
entre	between	*El museo está <u>entre</u> el cine y el parque.*
enfrente de	opposite	<u>*Enfrente del hotel*</u> *hay un monumento.*
frente a	opposite	<u>*Frente a*</u> *la tienda está mi casa.*
alrededor de	around	*No hay muchos bares <u>alrededor del</u> hotel.*
cerca de	near	<u>*Cerca del*</u> *hotel hay una agencia de viajes.*
lejos de	far	*El centro comercial queda <u>lejos de</u> la playa.*
debajo de	under	*La parada del autobús está <u>debajo de</u> ese puente.*
junto a	next to	*La estación del metro está <u>junto al</u> banco.*
aquí	here	<u>*Aquí*</u> *venden café.*
allí	there	<u>*Allí*</u> *no venden café.*

Places To Go in Mexico

The capital of Mexico, Mexico City, is known in Spanish as *la Ciudad de México*. However, you'll see it everywhere abbreviated as CDMX. CDMX is one of the main tourist destinations of Latin America.

To know more about CDMX, let's read a dialogue of a tourist who is a little lost in this huge city!

Turista: Disculpe, señora, ¿cómo puedo llegar al Museo Nacional de Antropología?

Señora: Eso está un poco lejos de aquí. Debe tomar la línea 2 del metro, la azul, en la estación Zócalo.

Turista: ¿Y dónde me bajo?

Señora: En la estación Hidalgo.

Turista: Parece muy sencillo. ¡Gracias!

Señora: ¡Espere, eso no es todo! Tiene que hacer un trasbordo y subirse al camión de la línea 7. El camión pasará por lugares emblemáticos de la ciudad, como el Ángel de la Independencia y el Museo de Arte Moderno.

Turista: Entiendo. ¿Y dónde me bajo?

Señora: La parada de autobús está justo

enfrente del Museo Nacional de
Antropología.

Surely you noticed that, in this conversation, the woman who gives directions to the tourist says the word *camión*. In most Spanish-speaking countries, *el camión* is a truck; however, in Mexico it's the word used to call the bus. (In any case, you can also say the words *bus* or *autobús*, and you'll be understood.)

Of course, Mexico City is only *one* of the thousands of destinations you have in Mexico. There are also beaches (among the most beautiful in the world, by the way). Some of the most important coastal cities are Cancun, Cozumel and Playa del Carmen.

Mexico is also home to many ancient indigenous cultures, such as the Aztecs (*los aztecas*) and the Mayans (*los mayas*). While the Mayans settled in what is now southeastern Mexico, the Aztec empire was in the center of the present-day Mexican territory. You can find incredible monuments of both civilizations throughout the country, like Chichén Itzá.

Vocabulary For Your Trip

Before moving on to the next chapter, let's see some more useful traveling vocabulary:

Spanish	English

la alberca	swimming pool
el ayuntamiento	city hall
bajarse (de un transporte)	to get off (of a transport)
el cajero automático	ATM
el camión	bus
la casa de cambio	currency exchange
la catedral	cathedral
el centro de la ciudad	city center, downtown
el crucero	cruise
el desayuno incluido	breakfast included
la estación de metro	subway station
la excursión	tour
la habitación (simple/doble)	room (single/double)
el huésped, la huésped	guest
la iglesia	church
el malecón	boardwalk
la media pensión	half board
el mar	sea
el metro	subway
la mochila	backpack

la montaña	mountain
el monumento	monument
el museo	museum
la oficina de información	information office
la propina	tip
el puerto	port
rentar (un departamento/un carro)	to rent (an apartment/a car)
la reserva	booking
subirse (a un transporte)	to get on (a transport)
tomar *(un transporte)*	to take (a transport)
el trasbordo	transfer
el tren	train
la parada de autobús	bus stop
el pasaporte	passport
la plaza principal	main square
la playa	beach

Key Takeaways

- There are many words that refer to our luggage. *El equipaje* is all of our things. *La maleta* is the suitcase we check, and *el bolso de mano* or *equipaje de mano* is the bag we carry with us.

- Normally, airlines allow suitcases weighing up to 50 pounds. In Mexico, they use kilos, and the equivalent is about 20 kg.

- In general, to ask for directions, sentences should begin in the following way:

¿Dónde está…?
¿Dónde hay…?
¿Dónde queda…?
¿Dónde es…?
¿Cómo llego a…?
¿Cómo puedo ir a…?
¿Cómo puedo llegar a…?

- Mexico City (known as CDMX) is one of the main destinations in Latin America. This great cosmopolitan city with a vibrant cultural life offers many tourist attractions. Other destinations in Mexico are the beaches, such as Cancun and Playa del Carmen, and the monuments of the Aztec and Mayan cultures.

We've talked about shopping and traveling, but we are missing one of the most enjoyable things in life... Yes, food! In chapter 8, we're going to see everything about Mexican food: how to order in a restaurant, how to say what we like and don't, and much more! But first, let's solve a few exercises.

Chapter Exercises

1. Fill in the blanks in this dialogue with one of these words: *aeropuerto, retrasado, tarjeta de embarque, libre de impuestos, escala, abordar, puerta de embarque.*

    A: Perdone, señorita, no puedo encontrar la _____ de mi vuelo. ¿Podría ayudarme?

    B: Por supuesto. Déjeme ver su _____.

    A: Aquí tiene.

    B: Veo que va a Monterrey y que tiene una _____ en Ciudad de México. Tiene que subir al segundo piso del

    _____.

    A: Muchas gracias. Entonces, iré a _____ el vuelo ahora mismo. ¡No quiero perderlo!

    B: No se preocupe: el vuelo está _____. Tiene tiempo para pasear por la zona _____ del aeropuerto.

2. In the next sentences, choose from the words in brackets to fill in the blanks.

a. En el Aeropuerto Internacional de la Ciudad de México operan muchísimas _____ (airolíneas/aerolíneas).

b. El uniforme de los _____ (aeromozos/aeromosos) es negro.

c. Necesito pasar por el mostrador de _____ (inmigraciones/migraciones).

d. Me encantaría viajar en _____ (primera clase/primero clase).

3. Match each Spanish word on the left with its English translation on the right.

   a. equipaje   1. handbag
   b. maleta   2. fanny pack
   c. bolso de mano   3. luggage
   d. riñonera   4. suitcase

4. In the next sentences, choose from the words in brackets to fill in the blanks.

   a. ¿Dónde _____ (hay/queda) un cajero automático?

   b. ¿Dónde _____ (hay/está) el centro de la ciudad?

   c. ¿Cómo _____ (llego/hago) a la playa?

   d. ¿Cómo puedo _____ (ir/estar) al museo?

5. Put the following dialogue in order.

   1) Claro. Tiene que tomar el autobús.

   2) De nada. ¡Buena suerte!

   3) Gracias.

4) ¿Dónde lo tomo?

5) Buenos días. Necesito llegar al centro de la ciudad. ¿Podría indicarme cómo ir?

6) En esa esquina de allí. El pasaje cuesta 10 pesos.

6. Read the following story and then answer the questions.

Santiago, un turista en Guadalajara, ha visitado la Basílica de Nuestra Señora de Zapopan y ahora quiere regresar al hotel. En la oficina de información de la basílica, una mujer le dijo: "Tómate la línea 3 del tren eléctrico y bájate en la estación Guadalajara Centro. Son solo seis estaciones desde aquí".

Las indicaciones de la mujer fueron bastante claras, así que Santiago está seguro de que no puede perderse. Se toma el tren y comienza a mirar por la ventana. Las vistas son muy bonitas. Después de algunos minutos, decide consultar un mapa de todas las estaciones de la red que hay sobre la puerta del vagón.

"¡Oh, no", piensa Santiago. "¡Estoy yendo hacia el otro lado!". Santiago se baja en la siguiente estación, llamada Mercado del Mar, y mira a su alrededor. Enfrente hay un parque muy bonito. "¡Quizá tomar el tren en la dirección contraria no haya sido tan malo!", piensa.

  a. Where is Santiago at the beginning of the story and where does he want to go?

  b. Where is the map with all the stations?

    c. At what station does Santiago get off? At what station should he have gotten off?

    d. How many train stations are there between Guadalajara Centro and the basilica?

7. Put the words in order to form coherent questions.

    a. el / queda / de / Arte / ¿Dónde / Museo / Moderno?

    b. puedo / un / comer? / ¿Dónde / lugar / encontrar / para

    c. playa? / a / llego / ¿Cómo / la

    d. está / diría / principal / ¿me / la / por / Disculpe, / plaza / pueblo, / dónde / del / favor?

8. In the following dialogue, choose from the words in brackets to fill in the blanks.

A: Buenos días, señorita. Quiero _____ (reserbar/reservar) una habitación solo para esta noche.

B: Por supuesto. ¿Una simple o una _____ (doble/double)?

A: Una simple, por favor. ¿Puede ser con _____ (vista/visión) al mar?

B: Lo siento, pero esas habitaciones están todas ocupadas. Pero tengo una bonita habitación con vista a la ciudad. ¡Es una de las más demandadas!

A: De acuerdo. Tomaré esa.

B: Estupendo. Aquí tiene su _____ (carta/tarjeta) para ingresar a la habitación. El _____ (desayuno/almuerzo)

se sirve en el comedor del hotel de 7 a 10. Tenga también un
_____ (mapa/mapo) de la ciudad. Si necesita algo puede
llamar a la _____ (resepción/recepción).

9. Decide whether the following statements about the dialogue
are true or false. Correct the false ones.

   a. La mujer quiere reservar una habitación doble.

   b. La mujer quiere hacer una reserva solo por una noche.

   c. El desayuno se sirve de 7 a 10 en el comedor del hotel.

   d. Todas las habitaciones con vista a la ciudad están
   ocupadas.

10. Choose from the adverbs and prepositions in brackets to fill
in the blanks.

   a. La iglesia está _____ (entre/debajo) el
   ayuntamiento y la tienda.

   b. _____ (Debajo/Cerca) de este hotel hay muchos
   restaurantes.

   c. Estamos un poco (_____ lejos/arriba) del
   aeropuerto.

   d. _____ (Entre/Junto a) la estación de trenes hay un
   supermercado.

Answer Key

1.

A: Perdone, señorita, no puedo encontrar la puerta de embarque de mi vuelo. ¿Podría ayudarme?

B: Por supuesto. Déjeme ver su tarjeta de embarque.

A: Aquí tiene.

B: Veo que va a Monterrey y que tiene una escala en Ciudad de México. Tiene que subir al segundo piso del aeropuerto.

A: Muchas gracias. Entonces, iré a abordar el vuelo ahora mismo. ¡No quiero perderlo!

2.

a. En el Aeropuerto Internacional de la Ciudad de México operan muchísimas aerolíneas.

b. El uniforme de los aeromozos es negro.

c. Necesito pasar por el mostrador de migraciones.

d. Me encantaría viajar en primera clase.

3.

a. equipaje 1. luggage

b. maleta 4. suitcase

c. bolso de mano 1. handbag

d. riñonera 2. fanny pack

4.

a. ¿Dónde hay un cajero automático?

b. ¿Dónde está el centro de la ciudad?

c. ¿Cómo llego a la playa?

d. ¿Cómo puedo ir al museo?

5.

5) Buenos días. Necesito llegar al centro de la ciudad. ¿Podría indicarme cómo ir? 1) Claro. Tiene que tomar el autobús.

4) ¿Dónde lo tomo?

6) En esa esquina de allí. El pasaje cuesta 10 pesos.

3) Gracias.

2) De nada. ¡Buena suerte!

6.

a. He is in the Basílica de Nuestra Señora de Zapopan and wants to go back to the hotel.

b. Above the coach door.

c. He gets off at Mercado del Mar, although he should have gotten off at Guadalajara Centro.

d. Six.

7.

a. ¿Dónde queda el Museo de Arte Moderno?

b. ¿Dónde puedo encontrar un lugar para comer?

c. ¿Cómo llego a la playa?

d. Disculpe, ¿me diría dónde está la plaza principal del pueblo, por favor?

8.

A: Buenos días, señorita. Quiero reservar una habitación

solo para esta noche.

B: Por supuesto. ¿Una simple o una doble?

A: Una simple, por favor. ¿Puede ser con vista al mar?

B: Lo siento, pero esas habitaciones están todas ocupadas. Pero tengo una bonita habitación con vista a la ciudad. ¡Es una de las más demandadas!

A: De acuerdo. Tomaré esa.

B: Estupendo. Aquí tiene su tarjeta para ingresar a la habitación. El desayuno se sirve en el comedor del hotel de 7 a 10. Tenga también un mapa de la ciudad. Si necesita algo puede llamar a la recepción.

9.

a. Falso. Ella quiere reservar una habitación simple.

b. Verdadero.

c. Verdadero.

d. Falso. Todas las habitaciones con vista al mar están ocupadas.

10.

a. La iglesia está entre el ayuntamiento y la tienda.

b. Cerca de este hotel hay muchos restaurantes.

c. Estamos un poco lejos del aeropuerto.

d. Junto a la estación de trenes hay un supermercado.

Chapter 8: *¿Te vas a comer eso?* Food and Eating Out

Las penas con pan son menos.

- Mexican proverb

Food is one of the most powerful cultural expressions there is. Everyone has a dish or a recipe that takes them right back to their childhood; taste and smell are really powerful when we're talking about recalling memories. You don't need to have watched *Ratatouille* to know that. When people gather at a table, something magical happens.

As you know, Mexican cuisine is well-known all around the world. You've probably eaten *tacos*, *nachos* or *burritos* more than once, and if you were lucky, they tasted great. But Mexican food is much more diverse than that. If you're planning a trip or a holiday, you are probably already excited about all the new food you're going to try. And that expectation is well justified. Mexican people take great pride in their food: every region has its own dishes, and even street food is quite creative.

That's why we want to make sure that you get the full experience. In this chapter, we're going to learn all about Mexican food—how to distinguish it, how to order it, and how to talk about it. To sum up, we're going to:

- discover the most common ingredients in Mexican food
- make a quick course in Mexican cuisine
- learn how to talk about likes, dislikes, restrictions and preferences
- understand how to order in a restaurant
- strengthen our grammar: it's present perfect time!

Common Ingredients

Japanese food has fish and rice; French food has cheese and butter; Italian food has flour, basil and tomatoes. Every cuisine, all over the world, has a few basic ingredients that, combined in different ways, give birth to different dishes. Mexican cuisine is no exception. That's why now we're going to make a list of some words that you'll find handy. We've divided the ingredients into categories to make it easier for you. You'll see that not all of them have a translation; some are called the same in English, and some just don't have an English word.

Vegetales (vegetables)

- *el ajo*: garlic.
- *el brócoli*: broccoli
- *la calabaza*: pumpkin.
- *la cebolla*: onion.
- *el chile*: chili.
- *el col*: cabbage.
- *los frijoles*: beans.
- *las habas*: fava beans.
- *la lechuga*: lettuce.
- *el nopal*: nopal (edible cactus).
- *la papa*: potato.
- *el rábano*: radish.
- *la zanahoria*: carrot.

Cereales (cereals)

- *el arroz*: rice:
- *la avena*: oat.
- *la cebada*: barley.
- *el centeno*: rye.
- *el maíz*: corn.
- *el trigo*: wheat.

Frutas (fruit)

- *la aceituna*: olive.
- *el aguacate*: avocado.
- *el durazno*: peach.
- *el jitomate*: tomato.
- *la lima*: lime.
- *el limón*: lemon.
- *el mango*: mango.
- *la manzana*: apple.
- *el pepino*: cucumber.
- *la pera*: pear.
- *la piña*: pineapple.
- *el plátano*: banana.

Frutos secos (nuts)

- *la almendra*: almond.
- *el cacahuate*: peanut.
- *la castaña*: chestnut.
- *la nuez*: nut.
- *el pistacho*: pistachio.

Hierbas y especias (herbs and spices)

- *la canela*: cinnamon.
- *el cilantro*: cilantro.
- *el clavo de olor*: clove.
- *el comino:* cumin.

- *el laurel*: laurel.
- *el orégano*: oregano.
- *el perejil*: parsley.
- *el pimentón*: paprika.
- *el pimiento*: pepper.

Lácteos (dairy products)

- *la crema*: cream.
- *la leche*: milk.
- *la manteca*: butter.
- *el queso*: cheese.
- *el yogur*: yogurt.

Carnes (meats)

- *el cerdo*: pork.
- *el pescado*: fish.
- *el pollo*: chicken.
- *la res*: beef.
- *los mariscos*: seafood.

Bebidas (drinks)

- *el agua*: water.
- *la cerveza*: beer.
- *la chela*: Mexican word for "beer".
- *el refresco*: soda.

- *el vino*: wine.

Otros (others)

- *el aceite*: oil.
- *el caldo*: broth.
- *la grasa*: fat.
- *el huevo*: egg.
- *la sal*: salt.
- *la salsa*: sauce.
- *la tortilla*: tortilla.

Mexican Dishes

Mexican food has hundreds and hundreds of dishes, each one more delicious than the next. Moreover, each region has its local specialty, from which every family has their own recipe. As you can imagine, the result could fill out a whole bookshelf (or more). Of course, we couldn't possibly make room for all of that. But we can make a sort of introductory course, focusing on dishes that are rather common, and that you can find in every restaurant all across Mexico. This will help you get a sense of Mexican cuisine. You won't be an expert, but you'll be a good *aficionado*. Are you ready? Let's get to it!

1. Los tacos

You surely know tacos. They are the most international Mexican food, and also one of the most versatile. Tacos are closer to a format than to a dish; you can make tacos of almost anything, as long as you use a hand-sized corn tortilla. That's why you can find thousands of fillings. Here's a short list of the most popular ones:

- *Al pastor*: beef grilled in a *trompo*—a rotating vertical spit similar to the one used to cook kebabs—with pineapple.
- *Cochinita pibil*: braised pork with *achiote*—a spice—cooked inside banana leaves.
- *Arrachera*: marinated grilled beef.
- *Birria*: braised mutton, marinated with tomato, chilies and spices.
- *Nopal*: edible cactus with cheese.
- *Al gobernador*: shrimp and peppers.
- *Quesadillas*: only cheese!

2. Los burritos

Burritos are mostly a to-go food: a tasty filling rolled in a large wheat tortilla. There are three main differences between the tortillas used for tacos and the ones used for burritos: the size, the fold and the flour. The filling can vary, but the most traditional one includes beef and *frijoles refritos* (fried beans).

3. Los totopos

Maybe you haven't heard of *totopos*, but I'm sure you know them. They have another name: nachos. They're not actually the same thing, but outside Mexico they tend to get confused. *Totopos* are any kind of fried corn tortilla, and are usually accompanied by a dip or a sauce; nachos are a particular dish that uses *totopos* and cheese.

4. Las enchiladas

Enchiladas are another street food classic. As you can guess from the name, they include a fair amount of chilis. This dish is basically a fried corn tortilla covered in spicy sauce and meat (or cheese, in some cases). So, the main difference between *enchiladas* and tacos is that enchiladas are spicy by definition, and that the tortilla is fried and not folded (of course, you can't fold a fried tortilla without breaking it).

5. El mole

A *mole* is basically a stew. The most famous one is the *mole poblano*, from the region of Puebla; it has a very long list of ingredients, but the main ones are chicken (or turkey), chilis (lots of them), spices, and different kinds of nuts. But there are almost 50 types of *mole* around Mexico, so be ready to be surprised!

6. El guacamole

Another international hit: the guacamole. You're probably familiar with this dish; it's basically a dip or sauce made of avocado, onion, and sometimes tomato. You can add it to your tacos or eat it with some *totopos*.

7. El pozole

A *pozole* is a strong broth made of corn. It usually has meat, lettuce and radish. Don't be fooled by its watery look—it's actually quite heavy. And spicy, of course.

8. Los tamales

Tamales are not exclusively Mexican—they are a Latinamerican dish. They can be found everywhere, from the Sonoran desert to the Patagonian steppe. They look like a very cute little package made with corn leaves (or sometimes *plátano* leaves). Inside, you'll find corn dough filled with meat or almost anything else. You can even find sweet ones!

9. Los chapulines

This dish is for adventurous people only. Well, in fact, *chapulines* are not actually a dish; they are more of an ingredient. And, if you're eating *chapulines*, you can't ignore them, because they are... grasshoppers. Mexicans usually fry them and eat them as a snack or inside a taco. It's not the only insect eaten in Mexico, but it's the most popular one.

10. Los chiles en nogada

This is one of the most representative dishes of Mexican cuisine. The main ingredient of *chiles en nogada* is, of course, chili. They are stuffed with a mix of meat and sweet fruits, fried, and then covered with *nogada*—a sauce made of nuts—and grains of pomegranate.

11. Los aguachiles

Aguachiles are basically the Mexican ceviche: shrimps marinated in lime with cilantro, red onion, and peppers.

12. Los chilaquiles

Do you remember *totopos*? Well, they are not only a side dish. They can also be breakfast! *Chilaquiles* are probably the most traditional Mexican breakfast: *totopos* with hot sauce and some protein, which can be meat or eggs. They are frequently covered with cheese or cream. In a way, they are very similar to *enchiladas*, but the presentation of the fried tortilla is different: instead of a whole tortilla, in *chilaquiles* you have small slices cut up in triangular shape (that is, *totopos*).

Talking about Food: Likes, Dislikes, Restrictions and Preferences

Now that you have a general idea of what Mexican food is like, we can start talking about what you like and dislike. We should also make sure that you can say all your dietary restrictions and allergies—we don't want you to have any unpleasant surprises! Let's take a deeper look into the world of food preferences.

Likes and Dislikes

As in English, in Spanish there are several ways of saying that you like something—and of course, there is an equally diverse group of ways of saying that you hate something. The main one is using the verb *gustar* ("to like") in a positive or negative way. Let's see a few examples:

- *Me gustan los tacos.* (I like tacos)
- *No me gusta el pescado.* (I don't like fish)
- *No me gustan los totopos.* (I don't like *totopos)*
- *Me gusta la salsa.* (I like the sauce)

We should point out two things. First, this verb doesn't agree with the person who likes or dislikes, but with the thing that is liked or disliked. We're saying something like "this thing is not likable to me." That's why, when we talk about *pescado* (singular) we say *gusta* (singular), but we say *gustan* (plural) when we talk about *tacos* (plural).

The second thing is that we always need a pronoun: *me*, if you are talking about yourself; *le*, if you are talking about a third person; *te*, if you are referring to the person you are talking to; *les*, if you are referring to two or more people. The pronoun determines which person we are talking about. This will become more clear with the example below.

We also have other verbs to talk about likes and dislikes. We can use *encantar* ("to like a lot"), *amar* ("to love") or *odiar* ("to hate"). Only *encantar* works in the same way as *gustar*; the other two are more similar to their English counterparts. Let's see a few examples:

- *Me encantan las enchiladas.* (I really like enchiladas)
- *A ella le encanta el pozole.* (She likes pozole a lot)
- *¿Te gusta la comida picante?* (Do you like spicy food?)
- *A mis hijos no les gusta desayunar.* (My children don't like having breakfast)
- *Él odia los chapulines.* (He hates chapulines)
- *Ellas odian el mole.* (They hate mole)
- *Amo este burrito.* (I love this burrito)
- *Nosotros amamos los aguachiles.* (We love aguachiles)

Restrictions and Allergies

We should also talk about the things that you don't want to eat. In order to do that, first we have to see a small list of handy vocabulary:

- *Vegetariano/a:* vegetarian.
- *Vegano/a*: vegan.
- *Celíaco/a, intolerante al gluten*: gluten-intolerant.
- *Alérgico/a a...* : allergic to....
- *Diabético/a*: diabetic.
- *Kosher*: kosher.
- *Halal*: halal.

- *Intolerante a...* : intolerant to...
- *Dieta:* diet.

As you can see, all these words are almost identical to their English counterparts. That's more than helpful, isn't it? But now we have to see how to use them. Luckily, it's not that hard, as it's mostly about using the verb *ser* or *estar*. Let's check it in a few examples:

- *Soy vegetariana.* (I'm vegetarian)
- *Soy alérgico al cacahuate.* (I'm allergic to peanuts)
- *Ella es intolerante a la lactosa.* (She's lactose-intolerant)
- *Ellos están a dieta.* (They're on a diet)

How to Order in a Restaurant

We're finally here. We've learned about Mexican food and we've studied how to express our likes, dislikes and restrictions. That means we're prepared for the ultimate test: to order food in a Mexican restaurant.

This is not particularly difficult. The waitstaff at a restaurant want you to order, and that means that they'll make an effort to overcome all language barriers. Many people just point at something on the menu and hope it turns out just fine. However, you won't need to do that, because in this section we'll teach you how to order something that you really fancy.

A conversation with a server will usually have two parts: first, you'll order the food, and then you'll pay for it—or at least you should! So let's focus on each of those parts.

How to Order

There are two verbs usually used for ordering food: *querer* ("to want") and *gustar* ("to like"). In this sense, it's not that different from English; we say "I want the tacos al pastor" or "I'd like the aguachiles". However, in Spanish we use a different tense for each verb: present tense for *querer* and conditional for *gustar*. Don't worry, we're not going to talk much about the conditional now—that's a whole other thing, and it's quite advanced. But we need to mention it so you can understand these examples:

- *Quiero los tacos al pastor, por favor.* (I want the tacos al pastor, please)
- *Me gustarían los aguachiles, por favor.* (I'd like the aguachiles, please)

As you can see, in this case the verb *gustar* is conjugated in quite a strange way. We're not going to focus on that; for now, take it as a useful phrase.

How to Pay

You've had dinner—hopefully, you've had a nice dinner—and now you have to go. Let's see how you can ask for the check:

- *La cuenta, por favor.* (The check, please)

That's it. Pretty easy, right? Before you leave the restaurant, there's one more thing: *la propina* ("the tip"). In Mexico, the tip tends to be between 10% and 15% of the bill.

A Conversation with a Waiter

As you know, ordering in a restaurant usually involves a few questions. The waiter will want to know what you're going to drink or how you like your meat, and you may want to ask how something is made. So here you have a short dialogue to get the flow of things:

Waiter: *Bienvenido. ¿En qué puedo ayudarlo?* (Welcome. How can I help you?)

Client: *Me gustaría ver el menú, por favor.* (I'd like to see the menu, please)

Waiter: *Aquí tiene.* (Here you have)

Client: *Gracias. Quiero los aguachiles, por favor.* (Thank you. I want the aguachiles, please)

Waiter: *Muy bien. ¿Y desea ordenar algo para beber?* (Very good. And would you like to order a drink?)

Client: *Me gustaría una cerveza.* (I'd like a beer)

Waiter: *Excelente, aguachiles y una cerveza. ¿Algo más?* (Excellent, aguachiles and a beer. Anything else?)

Client: *No, gracias. Disculpe, ¿los aguachiles tienen cacahuates? Soy alérgico.* (No, thanks. Excuse me, do the aguachiles have any peanuts? I'm allergic)

Waiter: *No, no tienen.* (No, they don't have any)

Client: *Excelente. ¡Muchas gracias!* (Excellent. Thank you very much!)

Key Takeaways

In this chapter we saw:

- the most common ingredients, from *aguacates* to *zanahorias*
- twelve very typical—and tasty—Mexican dishes
- how to talk about likes, dislikes and dietary restrictions
- how to order in a restaurant

Before moving on to chapter 9—one of the most fun in the book!—let's solve some exercises to apply everything you've learned.

Chapter Exercises

1. Fill in the blanks in this dialogue with one of these words:

   gustarían, hambre, quieres, vegetariana, preguntar.

A: ¿_____ comer algo, Julia?

B: Sí, me muero de _____. ¿Qué te parece ese puesto de

allí? Me _____ unos tacos al pastor.

A: ¿Creés que tendrán una opción _____?

B: No sé, pero podemos _____.

2. Match each dish with its description.

    a. Enchiladas   1. Fried pieces of corn tortilla.

    b. Pozole   2. Grasshoppers.

    c. Totopos   3. A fried tortilla with hot sauce and

    beef.

    d. Chapulines   4. A broth made of corn.

3. Fill in the blanks in these sentences about likes, dislikes and

    preferences with one of these words: *me gusta, vegetariano,*

    celíaca, odio.

    a. No como carne, pero sí queso. Soy _____.

    b. No puedo comer gluten. Soy _____.

    c. _____ la comida japonesa, pero prefiero la italiana.

    d. _____ el picante, no puedo soportarlo.

4. Conjugate the verbs in brackets in the correct tense. Add a pronoun if needed.

a. Los gatos no _____ (gustar).

b. A María _____ (gustar) los días lluviosos.

c. Nosotros _____ (odiar) las demoras.

d. A ellos _____ (encantar) salir de noche.

5. Which of the following sentences is grammatically correct?

a. Me gustarían comer unos totopos.

b. Los aguachiles están camarones con lima.

c. ¿Ese plato es muy picante?

d. No me gusta los tamales dulces.

6. Decide whether these sentences are true or false. Correct the false ones.

a. Los celíacos no pueden comer carne.

b. El pozole es una tortilla frita con carne y salsa picante.

c. Los chilaquiles se comen en el desayuno.

d. En México no se suele dejar propina.

7. Which of the following sentences is grammatically incorrect? Can you correct it?

a. Ayer comí un burrito horroroso, no me gustó nada.

b. No tengo hambre hoy.

c. ¿Quieres que pidamos la cuenta?

d. ¿Estos tacos tiene cilantro?

8. In the next sentences, choose from the words in brackets to fill in the blanks.

a. El restaurante _____ (abren/abre) a las ocho.

b. El guacamole lleva aguacate, chile y _____ (jitomate/pepino).

c. A mí no _____ (le/me) gusta el pescado.

d. Estas quesadillas _____ (están/son) frías.

9. Conjugate the verbs in brackets in the correct tense.

a. Ayer, en un restaurante nosotros _____ (encontrar) un pelo en la sopa.

b. Creo que yo ya _____ (tener) hambre.

c. Él no _____ (saber) qué era una enchilada.

d. _____ (ser) alérgica a los mariscos, no puedo comer camarones.

10. Now it's time for you to tell us (in Spanish!) your likes and dislikes.

a. ¿Cuál es tu plato favorito? _____

b. ¿Qué comida no soportas? _____

c. ¿Tienes alguna restricción alimentaria?

_____

d. ¿Comiste comida mexicana alguna vez? ¿Dónde?

_____

Answer Key

1.

A: ¿Quieres comer algo, Julia?

B: Sí, me muero de hambre. ¿Qué te parece ese puesto de allí? Me gustarían unos tacos al pastor.

A: ¿Creés que tendrán una opción vegetariana?

B: No sé, pero podemos preguntar.

2.

a. Enchilada   3. A fried tortilla with hot sauce and beef.

b. Pozole   4. A broth made of corn.

c. Totopos   1. Fried pieces of corn tortilla.

d. Chapulines   2. Grasshoppers.

3.

a. No como carne, pero sí queso. Soy vegetariano.

b. No puedo comer gluten. Soy celíaca.

c. Me gusta la comida japonesa, pero prefiero la italiana.

d. Odio el picante, no puedo soportarlo.

4.

a. Los gatos no me gustan.

b. A María le gustan los días lluviosos.

c. Nosotros odiamos las demoras.

d. A ellos les encanta salir de noche.

5.

c. ¿Ese plato es muy picante?

6.

a. False. Los celíacos no pueden comer gluten.

b. False. El pozole es un caldo.

c. True.

d. False. En México se suele dejar entre un 10% y un 15% de propina.

7.

d. ¿Estos tacos tienen cilantro?

8.

a. El restaurante abre a las ocho.

b. El guacamole lleva aguacate, chile y jitomate.

c. A mí no me gusta el pescado.

d. Estas quesadillas están frías.

9.

a. Ayer, en un restaurante nosotros encontramos un pelo en la sopa.

b. Creo que yo ya tengo hambre.

c. Él no sabía qué era una enchilada.

d. Soy alérgica a los mariscos, no puedo comer camarones.

Chapter 9: ¡Música, maestro!

Hay que llenar el planeta de violines y guitarras en lugar de tanta metralla.

- Chavela Vargas

Before you start reading this chapter, we have a recommendation for you: put a song that you really like in the background (it's better if it's in Spanish!). Are you ready? Let's get started!

You probably know more than one popular Mexican song. "La Cucaracha", for example, is one of the most famous. But Mexican musical culture goes way beyond that, of course. Mexicans love music (who doesn't, anyway?), so we thought it was important for you to learn a few things about it. In this chapter, we will explore:

- Mexican musical genres
- preferences: how to talk about your musical taste
- the instruments in Spanish
- how to sing "Happy Birthday" in Mexico
- and a lot of music-related vocabulary.

Let's take it from the top!

Mexican Musical Genres

Current Mexican music is the result of a mix between European and American traditions, but it also has deep pre-Hispanic and African roots. This is, indeed, what makes it very special, and it's the reason why Mexico has many different typical instruments.

One of the most important Mexican musical genres is the *mariachi*. A *mariachi* band consists of a musical group made up of at least three people who play the guitar, the trumpet and the violin, and who perform traditional Mexican songs. *Mariachis* are a very important cultural element in Mexico, so don't be surprised if you see a group of them at any social event!

Of course, *mariachi* is not the only Mexican musical genre. *Cumbia* is also very popular over there, and it has been since the late 1950s. Probably, one of the most iconic Mexican *cumbia* singers was Selena, who popularized songs like "Como la flor".

Finally, we can't ignore the *boleros*. This genre is Cuban, but it was popularized in Mexico with singers like Luis Miguel. Generally, *boleros* tell stories of love and heartbreak, and the musicians play the guitar, the trumpet and the piano.

Let's see, we've already mentioned *mariachi*, *cumbia* and *boleros*... but there's more! Let's take a look at this list of typical Mexican musical genres:

Musical genre	Characteristics
El mariachi	It has at least three members. They play the guitar, the trumpet and the violin.
La cumbia	It's the Mexican version of Colombian *cumbia*. It has electric guitar, *congas*, saxophone and *güiro*.
Los boleros	It was originally Cuban, but it has extended to Mexico. Its lyrics are usually romantic.
La ranchera	It's part of Mexican folk music. Chavela Vargas was one of its greatest exponents.
El grupero	It was born in the late 1990s. It uses synthesizers and electronic instruments.
El rock mexicano	Mexico has one of the most important rock scenes in Latin America. The most common instruments are the electric guitar and the drums.
La música urbana	In recent years, urban music has proliferated in Mexico, and rap and reggaeton singers have risen to fame.

Preferences: How to Talk About Your Taste in Music

The music we like is something important. In our teenage years, it defines our friend group, and when we grow up, we can use music to start a conversation. But how do we talk about our musical taste? Well, it's not that different from talking about food. Some constructions we can use are the following:

- *Me gusta...* (I like...)
- *No me gusta...* (I don't like...)
- *Me encanta...* (I love...)
- *Prefiero...* (I prefer...)
- *Me interesa.../Estoy interesado/a en...* (I'm interested in...)

Now, let's look at some dialogues. You will see that there are some typical questions to find out about someone's musical taste, and also some possible answers.

- *¿Qué tipo de música te gusta?* (What kind of music do you like?)
- *Me gustan las rancheras.* (I like rancheras)

- *¿Qué música escuchas?* (What kind of music do you listen to?)
- *Escucho cumbia.* (I listen to cumbia)

- *¿Cuál es tu banda favorita?* (What's your favorite band?)

- *Mi banda favorita es Maná.* (My favorite band is Maná)

- *¿Qué música prefieres?* (What kind of music do you prefer?)
- *Prefiero los boleros.* (I prefer boleros)

- *¿Quién es tu cantante preferido?* (Who is your favorite singer?)
- *Mi cantante preferido es Luis Miguel.* (My favorite singer is Luis Miguel)

- *¿Qué música te gusta más?* (What kind of music do you like the most?)
- *Me gusta la música pop.* (I like pop music)

Playing an Instrument

In Spanish, the verb we use to say that we play an instrument is *tocar*. This is an irregular verb of the first conjugation (the ones ending in AR), but the irregularity only appears when the "C" ends up before an "E". In these cases, the "C" becomes a "QU". Let's see this verb conjugated in the main tenses.

	Presente	*Pretérito perfecto*	*Pretérito imperfecto*	*Futuro simple*
Yo	*toco*	*toqué*	*tocaba*	*tocaré*

Tú	tocas	tocaste	tocabas	tocarás
Él/ella	toca	tocó	tocaba	tocará
Nosotros/ nosotras	tocamos	tocamos	tocábamos	tocaremos
Ustedes (*)	tocan	tocaron	tocaban	tocarán
Ellos/ ellas	tocan	tocaron	tocaban	tocarán

Two other important verbs we'll need to talk about instruments are *aprender* ("to learn") and *enseñar* ("to teach").

Let's take a look at an example dialogue:

A: ¿**Tocas** algún instrumento?

B: Sí, **toco** el piano. Mi padre nos enseñó a mi hermana y a mí. En casa, siempre lo **tocábamos** hasta tarde. ¿Y tú? ¿**Tocas** algún instrumento?

A: No. Me gustaría aprender a **tocar** el saxofón. Mi abuelo lo **tocaba** cuando era joven.

B: ¿Y ya no lo **toca**?

A: No, ¡ahora está aprendiendo a **tocar** el bandoneón!

Musical Instruments: Vocabulary

In Spanish, many musical instruments have the same root as their English translation, such as *guitarra* ("guitar"), *saxofón* ("saxophone") and *flauta* ("flute"). Others are actually spelled the same, like *piano* or *violín* (well, almost the same: in Spanish you have to add an accent mark on the final "I"). You will also find some traditional instruments, such as the *güiro*, that doesn't really have an English translation.

Here's a list of the main instruments used in Mexican music.

Musical instrument	English translation
Instrumentos de cuerda ("string instruments")	
la guitarra	guitar
la guitarra eléctrica	electric guitar
el bajo	bass guitar
el guitarrón	*guitarrón*
el violín	violin
el piano	piano
Instrumentos de viento ("wind instruments")	
el saxofón	saxophone
la flauta	flute
el clarinete	clarinet
la trompeta	trumpet
Instrumentos de percusión ("percussion instruments")	

la batería	drums
el güiro	*güiro*
los platillos	cymbals
el bombo	bass drum

Happy Birthday to You!

We don't want to finish this chapter without talking about one of the most iconic songs in Mexico: "Las mañanitas". Although "Cumpleaños feliz" (the Spanish-speaking version of the classic "Happy Birthday to You") is also used, "Las mañanitas" is definitely the song that all Mexicans sing over a birthday cake.

These are the lyrics: *Estas son las mañanitas que cantaba el rey David / Hoy por ser día de tu santo te las cantamos aquí.* (This is the morning song that King David sang / Because today is your saint's day we're singing it to you)

Music Related Vocabulary

Finally, it's time to add a few new terms to your vocabulary. Let's see some Mexican Spanish words that are related to music.

Spanish	English
la canción	song

el sencillo	single
el disco	disc
el cantante, la cantante	singer
la banda	band
el grupo	group
el intérprete, la intérprete	interpreter
el vocalista, la vocalista	vocalist
el guitarrista, la guitarrista	guitarist
el baterista, la baterista	drummer
el saxofonista, la saxofonista	saxophonist
el coro	choir
el cantautor, la cantautora	singer-songwriter
la letra	lyrics
el estribillo	chorus
el escenario	stage
el solista, la solista	soloist
el dúo	duet
el cuarteto	quartet

Key Takeaways

Let's review what we've learned in this chapter:

- Mexican music has European, American, pre-Hispanic and African roots.
- Some of the most popular musical genres in Mexico are *mariachi, cumbia, boleros*, and *rancheras*.
- To talk about your musical taste, you can say *me gusta, no me gusta, me encanta, prefiero,* and *me interesa* or *estoy interesado/a en*.
- The verb used to talk about playing instruments is *tocar*.
- Some of the most important musical instruments are *guitarra* ("guitar"), *piano* ("piano"), *saxofón* ("saxophone"), and *trompeta* ("trumpet").
- In Mexico, before blowing the candles in a birthday party, they sing "Las mañanitas".

Now, a quick question for you: when do we usually listen to a lot of music? Exactly: during the holidays! In the next chapter, we are going to see everything about Mexican holidays (from the Day of the Dead to the famous Cinco de Mayo). But before that, we leave you with a few exercises to put what you've learned in this chapter to the test.

Chapter Exercises

1. From the following list, select a Mexican singer or band and choose one of their songs: Maná - Juan Gabriel - Julieta

Venegas - Thalía - Café Tacvba. After listening to it, answer these questions in Spanish.

    a. What is the song about?

    b. What genre would you say the song belongs to?

    c. Do you distinguish the instruments played in the song?

    d. What is your favorite part of the lyrics?

2. Decide whether the following statements are true or false. Correct the false ones.

    a. Mariachis use electric guitars.

    b. Luis Miguel is known for singing boleros.

    c. Selena is one of the most iconic Mexican cumbia singers.

    d. Tango is a Mexican genre.

3. Fill in the blanks with one of the following words: *sencillo, saxofonista, canción, dúo, pianista.*

    a. El _____ toca el saxofón y la pianista toca el _____.

    b. Jesse & Joy son un _____ de pop.

c. El _____ suele ser la principal canción en un disco.

d. El estribillo de esa _____ es muy pegadizo.

4. Which of the following sentences is grammatically correct?

    a. Me encanta las rancheras.

    b. Me encantan las rancheras.

    c. Me encanta las ranchera.

    d. Me encantan la ranchera.

5. In the next dialogue, choose from the words in brackets to fill in the blanks.

A: ¿Qué música te _____ (encanta/gusta) más?

B: Escucho de todo, aunque últimamente _____ (prefiero/prefería) las rancheras. ¿Y tú?

A: A mí me _____ (gusta/gustar) mucho el rock. Una de mis _____ (bandos/bandas) favoritas es Molotov. ¿Los conoces?

B: Por supuesto. Me _____ (encantan/encanta) Molotov. Tengo todos sus _____ (discos/discas) y sé todas sus _____ (canciones/estribillos).

A: ¿Neta? Entonces, ¿quieres ir al _____ (concierto/concerto) conmigo?

6. Match each question on the left with its answer on the right.

a. ¿Te gusta el rock?   1.   La cumbia.

b. ¿Qué música te gusta más?   2.   ¡Me encanta!

c. ¿Tocas algún instrumento?   3. El pop.

d. ¿Prefieres la cumbia o las rancheras?   4.   Sí,   la batería.

7. Fill in the blanks with the correct conjugation of the verb *tocar*.

   a. Mi abuela _____ el piano en su juventud.

   b. El vecino siempre _____ la batería hasta muy tarde.

   c. Estoy nerviosa porque mañana _____ el saxofón ante un público muy grande.

   d. En mi familia, todos _____ algún instrumento.

8. Put the following instruments into the corresponding group according to whether they are string (*cuerda*), wind (*viento*) or percussion (*percusión*) instrumentos: *batería, tambor, guitarra, flauta, trompeta, ukelele, maracas, guitarrón, violín, clarinete, tuba, timbales.*

a. Instrumentos de cuerda: _____, _____, _____, _____.

b. Instrumentos de viento: _____, _____, _____, _____.

c. Instrumentos de percusión: _____, _____, _____, _____.

9. Read the following news article. Then, answer the questions.

El mariachi es oficialmente Patrimonio de la Humanidad

La Unesco declaró al mariachi como Patrimonio Inmaterial de la Humanidad, en el marco del XIX Encuentro Internacional de Guadalajara.

El reconocimiento tuvo lugar este lunes durante un breve acto realizado en la plaza pública de Guadalajara. Allí, la directora del Consejo Nacional para la Cultura y las Artes de México (CONACULTA) entregó un premio simbólico a un grupo de ocho niños músicos de entre 5 y 10 años.

Durante el acto, un grupo de 13 mariachis cantó "El son de la negra", una de las melodías más emblemáticas de este género, para celebrar la decisión.

a. Where did the ceremony take place?

    b. Who received the award?

    c. How many mariachis performed during the act?

    d. Why did the mariachis sing "El son de la negra"?

10. Now, it is time for you to tell us (in Spanish!) what kind of music you like.

    a. ¿Qué   tipo   de   música   escuchas?
       _____.

    b. ¿Cuál es tu banda favorita? _____.

    c. ¿A   qué   concierto   te   gustaría   ir?
       _____.

    d. ¿Qué instrumento te encantaría poder tocar?
       _____.

Answer Key

2.

a. False. They use classic guitars.

b. True.

c. True.

d. False. Tango is an Argentinian genre.

3.

a. El saxofonista toca el saxofón y la pianista toca el piano.

b. Jesse & Joy son un dúo de pop.

c. El sencillo suele ser la principal canción en un disco.

d. El estribillo de esa canción es muy pegadizo.

4.

b. Me encantan las rancheras.

5.

A: ¿Qué música te gusta más?

B: Escucho de todo, aunque últimamente prefiero las rancheras. ¿Y tú?

A: A mí me gusta mucho el rock. Una de mis bandas favoritas es Molotov. ¿Los conoces?

B: Por supuesto. Me encanta Molotov. Tengo todos sus discos y sé todas sus canciones.

A: ¿Neta? Entonces, ¿quieres ir al concierto conmigo?

6.

a. ¿Te gusta el rock? 2. ¡Me encanta!

b. ¿Qué música te gusta más? 3. El pop

c. ¿Tocas algún instrumento? 4, Sí, la batería

c. ¿Prefieres la cumbia o las rancheras? 1. La cumbia

7.

a. Mi abuela tocaba el piano en su juventud.

b. El vecino siempre toca la batería hasta muy tarde.

c. Estoy nerviosa porque mañana tocaré el saxofón ante un público muy grande.

d. En mi familia, todos tocan algún instrumento.

8.

a. Instrumentos de cuerda: guitarra, ukelele, guitarrón, violín

b. Instrumentos de viento: flauta, trompeta, clarinete, tuba

c. Instrumentos de percusión: batería, tambor, maracas, timbales

9.

a. In the public square of Guadalajara.

b. A group of eight child musicians.

c. Thirteen.

d. Because it's one of the most emblematic songs of the genre.

Chapter 10: *¡Viva México!* Festivities and Special Days

Todo en México tiene para mí una fuerza secreta que me seduce. Su tradición y su esperanza en el futuro, la vida de su pueblo, la riqueza de su paisaje.

- Alfredo Zalce

Good food, friends and family, music and beer. Who doesn't like the holidays, after all? Like every country in the world, Mexico has some special dates on its calendar. Day of the Dead, Cinco de Mayo and September 16th are just some of this country's holidays. But do you know what Mexicans celebrate on these days? And what do they do to celebrate?

In this chapter, we'll talk about:

- the future tense
- Mexican festivities
- how to greet on special days

Future Tense

Before talking about festivities, we will briefly talk about the future tenses of verbs in Spanish. To talk about the future, in Spanish we use the *futuro simple* ("simple future"). For example:

- *Festejaré el Día de Muertos con mi familia.* (I will celebrate the Day of the Dead with my family)
- *Mis amigos y yo viajaremos a Cancún para festejar el Día de la Independencia.* (My friends and I will travel to Cancún to celebrate Independence Day)
- *Mi novia me dijo que me regalará un libro por Navidad.* (My girlfriend told me she will give me a book for Christmas)
- *¿Vendrás esta noche a la fiesta de Año Nuevo, carnal?* (Will you come tonight to the New Year's Eve party, mate?)

Now, let's see how to conjugate verbs in the *futuro simple*. For regular verbs of the first, second and third conjugation (those that end in AR, ER and IR, respectively), the formula is quite simple: the verb followed by the corresponding ending:

yo		-é
tú		-ás
él/ella	the verb	-á
nosotros/as		-emos
ustedes		-án

			-án
ellos/as			

Let's see a table with the conjugation of three verbs that fit very well with this chapter...

	Festejar ("to celebrate")	Beber ("to drink")	Compartir ("to share")
Yo	festejar**é**	beber**é**	compartir**é**
Tú	festejar**ás**	beber**ás**	compartir**ás**
El/ella	festejar**á**	beber**á**	compartir**á**
Nosotros/ nosotras	festejar**emos**	beber**emos**	compartir**emos**
Ustedes	festejar**án**	beber**án**	compartir**án**
Ellos/ellas	festejar**án**	beber**án**	compartir**án**

By the way: In Mexico, as in many other Hispanic countries, it is common to use a phenomenon known as *perífrasis* to talk about the future. It consists of the replacement of the *futuro simple* by the construction of the verb *ir* ("to go") followed by the preposition *a*, and then the infinitive of the verb. For example: *iré* ("I'll go") becomes *voy a ir*; *comeré* ("I'll eat") becomes *voy a comer* and *viajaré* ("I'll travel") becomes *voy a viajar*.

Now that we have seen how to conjugate verbs in the future tense, it's time to talk about Mexican holidays. And we'll start with one of the most important: the Day of the Dead!

El Día de Muertos

Let's look at a dialogue where verbs are used in the future tense. Then, we'll see the history of the Day of the Dead.

> A: ¡Feliz Día de Muertos!
>
> B: Gracias e igualmente para ti. ¿Cómo lo **festejarás**?
>
> A: Como siempre: mi familia y yo **pondremos** un altar en nuestra casa. **Haremos** ofrendas de pan de muerto y calaveritas de azúcar. Luego, **iremos** al cementerio, **decoraremos** las lápidas de nuestros seres queridos y **honraremos** su memoria. ¿Y tú?
>
> B: Yo **participaré** del Festival de las Calaveras en Aguascalientes. **Iré** junto a mi esposa. Nos **vamos a disfrazar** de calaveras y **vamos a honrar** a nuestros difuntos con alegría.

Each year, on November 1 and 2, Mexico celebrates the *Día de Muertos* ("Day of the Dead"), a holiday in which the memory of the deceased is honored. It originated from the union of the Catholic religion and the various indigenous cultures of Mexico.

The *Día de Muertos* is celebrated throughout Mexico and in regions of many other countries in the Americas, from Argentina to the United States. However, the way of celebrating it changes from place to place. In Mexico City, the festivities begin on October 31, with the cleaning and decoration of mausoleums and stones. In

Aguascalientes, they have the *Festival de las Calaveras* ("Skull Festival"), an event in which the inhabitants commemorate their deceased with parades and costumes.

Día de la Independencia

In the early hours of September 16, 1810, the priest Miguel Hidalgo Costilla rang the bells of the church in the city of Dolores to gather the citizens and motivate them to rise against the Spanish Crown. Finally, on September 27, 1821, Mexico became a free and sovereign country.

In Mexico, Independence Day celebrations start on the night of September 15. Many emblematic buildings in the cities are lit up with the colors of the Mexican flag, and people go to the main squares of the cities to enjoy the fireworks and eat typical dishes.

During this time of the year, you can hear a phrase that sums up the spirit of unity and the strong sense of identity of Mexicans: *¡Viva México!* (Long live Mexico!)

Cinco de Mayo

Finally, we have *Cinco de Mayo,* another special day in Mexico… and outside the country as well! This day, Mexicans around the world commemorate the victory of the Mexican army over the French army in the Battle of Puebla, on May 5, 1862. Well, the story of this battle is quite interesting.

A year before the battle, the Mexican government was facing many economic problems. It had large debts with several European countries, including France. With the intention of negotiating, France arrived in Mexico with around 6,000 soldiers (you can imagine that the negotiation was just an excuse). With barely 2,000 men, Mexico defended against the attack and won.

There's a fun fact about this holiday: in Mexico, outside the city of Puebla people don't celebrate *Cinco de Mayo*. Actually, it's a day particularly celebrated by the Mexican community in the United States, where it's a symbolic date in which they celebrate their Mexican identity.

Other Mexican Holidays

Although the ones above are the most famous, there are many other holidays in Mexico:

La Guelaguetza

It's celebrated every summer in the city of Oaxaca. Sixteen ethnic groups that live in that state come together, and each one offers its dances and its culture to the others. It is a super fun and colorful party!

Día de la Revolución Mexicana

November 20 marks the Day of the Mexican Revolution, an armed conflict that began in 1910. It's considered one of the most important political and social events in Latin America. The revolution sought, among other things, an agrarian reform that would benefit peasants and indigenous people.

Fiesta de la Candelaria

La Candelaria is a Catholic holiday celebrated on February 2. On this day, Mexicans eat a lot of tamales, a food of pre-Columbian origin consisting of corn dough filled with vegetables, meat, sauce and other ingredients.

Holiday Greetings

How to greet someone on a special date? In most of the festivities, you can begin the phrase with the word *Feliz...* ("Happy/Merry..."):

- *Feliz Día de Muertos*
- *Feliz Día de la Independencia*
- *Feliz Cinco de Mayo*

However, for *Pascuas* ("Easter") and *Fiestas* (both Christmas and New Year), which are plural words, we'll say *Felices*:

- *Felices Pascuas*
- *Felices Fiestas*

To answer to the greeting, we can say:

- *Gracias*
- *Igualmente*
- *Igual para ti*
- *Lo mismo para ti*

Key Takeaways

- To talk about the future, we use *futuro simple*, which is formed by the infinitive of the verb followed by the corresponding ending.
- It's also common to use a *perífrasis*, which consists of the verb *ir* ("to go") followed by the preposition "a" and an infinitive verb.
- In Mexico there are many festivities. Some of the most important are:
  - Día de Muertos
  - Cinco de Mayo
  - La Guelaguetza
  - Día de la Revolución
  - La Candelaria
- To wish someone a happy holiday, you have to say *Feliz* followed by the name of the holiday.
- The answers are *¡gracias!* or *igualmente*

And that's it! You've managed to finish this book on Mexican Spanish! *¡Felicitaciones!* Before saying goodbye, let's do one last set of exercises.

Chapter Exercises

1. Conjugate the verbs in brackets in the simple future.
    A: ¿Cómo _____ (festejar) el Día de la Independencia?
    B: Mi familia y yo _____ (ir) al Zócalo. ¿Tú también _____ (ir)?
    A: No. Yo _____ (viajar) a Chihuahua a visitar unos familiares. _____ (volver) la próxima semana.

2. Fill in the blanks with the corresponding ending to form the *futuro simple*.

    a. Yo viajar___ a Aguascalientes.

    b. Ella festejar___ el Día de la Independencia con su madre.

    c. Mi familia y yo partir___ a Puebla mañana para festejar el Cinco de Mayo.

    d. Mis primos participar___ de un desfile por el Día de Muertos.

3. The following verbs are conjugated in the *futuro simple*. Can you transform them to the periphrasis *ir + a +* the infinitive?

a. Yo bailaré → Yo voy a bailar

b. Tú viajarás →

c. Ella celebrará →

d. Ustedes beberán →

4. Can you translate the following words into English?

   a. Calavera

   b. Lápida

   c. Honrar

   d. Difuntos

5. Fill in the blanks with one of the following words: *personas, finales, alegremente, celebración, culto.* La Guelaguetza es una _____ que tiene lugar en el estado de Oaxaca a _____ de julio. Esta fecha rinde _____ a la Virgen del Carmen. En esta fiesta se pueden ver _____ con trajes típicos bailando _____.

6. Decide whether the following statements about Cinco de Mayo are true or false.

   a. Cinco de Mayo is celebrated in every corner of Mexico.

b. Cinco de Mayo commemorates a battle between Mexico and Spain.

c. The battle of Puebla was in 1862.

d. The French brought an army of 6,000 men to Mexico.

7. The following text about Independence Day has several grammatical and orthographic errors. Can you correct them?

El Día de la Independensia de México se celebra el 16 de septiembre. Sin embargo, lo festejos comiensan la noche anterior. Cerca de las once de las noche, los mexicanos se reúnen en la plazas más importante del país para esperar por el nuebo día. Durante el día 16, los personas festejan con bailes, comida y desfile.

8. In the following news article, conjugate the verbs in brackets in the simple future.

_____ **el Día de la Independencia en el Ángel**

Esta semana, los habitantes de la Ciudad de México _____ (festejar) una nueva conmemoración del Grito de la Independencia. Para ello, las autoridades locales han decidido que _____ (cortar) las calles circundantes al Ángel de la Independencia.

Los festejos _____ (comenzar) a partir de las diez de la noche, por lo que los dueños de comercios de la zona _____ (cerrar) sus puertas alrededor de las nueve.

9. Correct the following sentences.

    a. La Guelaguetza se festeja en invierno.

    b. El Día de la Revolución Mexicana conmemora la Independencia de México ante España.

    c. En la fiesta de La Candelaria, es común comer tacos.

    d. Miguel Hidalgo Costilla hizo sonar las campanas en la iglesia de la ciudad de Oaxaca.

10. Fill in the blanks with *Feliz* or *Felices*.

    a. _____ fiestas de La Candelaria.

    b. Que pases un _____ Día de la Independencia.

    c. Te deseo unas _____ Navidades.

    d. Que tengas un _____ Cinco de Mayo.

Answer Key

1.

A: ¿Cómo festejarás el Día de la Independencia?

B: Mi familia y yo iremos al Zócalo. ¿Tú también irás?

A: No. Yo viajaré a Chihuahua a visitar unos familiares. Volveré la próxima semana.

2.

    a. Yo viajaré a Aguascalientes.

    b. Ella festejará el Día de la Independencia con su madre.

c. Mi familia y yo partiremos a Puebla mañana para festejar el Cinco de Mayo.

d. Mis primos participarán de un desfile por el Día de Muertos

3.

a. Yo bailaré → Yo voy a bailar

b. Tú viajarás → Tu vas a viajar

c. Ella celebrará → Ella va a celebrar

d. Ustedes beberán → Ustedes van a beber

4.

a. Calavera: skull

b. Lápida: gravestone

c. Honrar: to honor

d. Difuntos: deceased

5.

La Guelaguetza es una celebración que tiene lugar en el estado de Oaxaca a finales de julio. Esta fecha rinde culto a la Virgen del Carmen. En esta fiesta se pueden ver personas con trajes típicos bailando alegremente.

6.

    a. False

    b. False

    c. True

    d. True

7.

El Día de la Independencia de México se celebra el 16 de septiembre. Sin embargo, los festejos comienzan la noche anterior. Cerca de las once de la noche, los mexicanos se reúnen en las plazas más importantes del país para esperar por el nuevo día. Durante el día 16, las personas festejan con bailes, comida y desfiles.

8.

Festejarán el Día de la Independencia en el Ángel Esta semana, los habitantes de la Ciudad de México festejarán una nueva conmemoración del Grito de la Independencia. Para ello, las autoridades locales han decidido que cortarán las calles circundantes al Ángel de la Independencia. Los festejos comenzarán a partir de las diez de la noche, por lo que los dueños de comercios de la zona cerrarán sus puertas alrededor de las nueve.

9.

    a. La Guelaguetza se festeja en verano.

    b. El Día de la Revolución Mexicana conmemora un conflicto armado que empezó en 1910.

    c. En la fiesta de La Candelaria, es común comer tamales.

    d. Miguel Hidalgo Costilla hizo sonar las campanas en la iglesia de la ciudad de Dolores.

10.

    a. Felices fiestas de La Candelaria.

    b. Que pases un Feliz Día de la Independencia.

    c. Te deseo unas Felices Navidades.

    d. Que tengas un Feliz Cinco de Mayo.

Conclusion

¡Felicitaciones, güey!

You've reached the end of this book, and we're very happy about it. Throughout 10 chapters, you've learned some of the most important aspects of Mexican Spanish, and we love having been part of that process.

How about we do a review of everything we've talked about? Let's see...

In the first chapter, we decided to bring you some basic notions to start any conversation in Spanish. We started by exploring Spanish greetings (those that go beyond *hola*), such as *buenos días, buenas tardes, buenas noches, ¿qué tal?, ¿cómo te va?* and more. Then, we focused on saying goodbye, from *adiós* to *hasta luego*, including the very Mexican way *adiosito*. Finally, we studied the correct words to speak politely: *por favor, gracias, disculpe, perdón* and more. In the grammar section, we saw the present tense.

In chapter 2, we talked about interrogations, both open questions (wh-questions, those that start with *qué, cuál, quién, cómo, cuándo, dónde* and *por qué*) and closed questions (the ones we can answer with yes or no). We also looked at gender and number in Spanish nouns, and we learned why agreement is so important.

Chapter 3 was dedicated to Mexican Spanish. We saw a few differences between the Spanish of Spain (also known as European Spanish or standard Spanish) and the one spoken in Mexico. One of the most important ones is the pronoun for the second person plural: while in Spain they use *vosotros*, in Mexico they use *ustedes*. But of course that's not the only difference. There are many everyday words that are different in Mexico and Spain. That's why we made a complete list in which we presented lots of words in Mexican Spanish, and their equivalents in standard Spanish.

In the fourth chapter, we talked about jobs and careers. We gave you an extensive list of professions and jobs, and we also looked at some common dialogues about work. In the grammar section, we introduced the simple past tense. After that grammar section, we had some fun! In chapter 5, we explored a bunch of typical phrases and idioms that are widely used in Mexico.

In chapter 6, we taught you how to go shopping in all kinds of places: malls, thrift stores, and flea markets. We also looked at some grammar: the *pretérito imperfecto*, a verb tense used to talk about an indeterminate past. Finally, we saw a bunch of useful shopping vocabulary like *caro*, *barato*, *oferta* or *descuento*.

The seventh chapter is undoubtedly one of the most important. Here, we saw all the phrases and words we need to get around an airport, from asking where the gate is to knowing how to get to the airport food court. In this chapter, we also saw how to ask for directions on the streets of Mexico. Finally, we've looked at those places that you can't miss on your trip to this wonderful country: its main city, the paradisiacal beaches, the Aztec and Mayan ruins, and much more.

Chapter 8 whets anyone's appetite, because in this chapter we talked about everything related to Mexican food. What are the typical Mexican dishes? Which condiments do they use? How do I make some real *enchiladas*? We also gave all the necessary vocabulary to communicate fluently with a waiter or waitress in Mexico. We taught you how to order food, how to ask for the bill, and how to talk about any dietary restrictions.

In chapter 9, we covered Mexican music. We explained how to talk about your musical preferences, and we saw what the main musical instruments are in Spanish music. In addition, we learned about the most important music genres in Mexico (*mariachi, boleros, rancheras, cumbias*...).

In the last chapter, we talked about the most important festivities in Mexico. Of course, we mentioned the Day of the Dead and Independence Day, perhaps two of the most well-known Mexican holidays. But, in addition, we looked at interesting facts about other regional holidays, such as La Candelaria or La Guelaguetza. We also learned how to greet people during those days.

Finally, we got to the end of the book, but also to the beginning of a new journey: that of speaking Spanish like a native! The next thing to do is go out into the world and practice, practice, and practice! Meanwhile, we're sure this guide will be a great ally.

¡Adiosito!

Book Description

Do you want to learn to speak Mexican Spanish in 30 days? Keep reading...

Are you planning a trip to Mexico and want to learn Spanish? Do you know a few words in that language, but you feel it's not enough? All the books you have seen are about European Spanish, but do you want to learn the one spoken in Mexico?

If you want to immerse yourself in real Mexican Spanish, then this book is for you!

You see, learning to speak Spanish like they do in Mexico shouldn't be that difficult. Actually, it's simpler than you thought.

Learn Mexican Spanish for Adult Beginners Workbook: Speak Mexican Spanish in 30 Days! is an excellent guide that'll teach you everything you need to know about Mexican Spanish.

With this book, you'll learn:

- To begin and maintain a conversation
- The differences between European and Mexican Spanish
- Lots of idioms and typical Mexican expressions
- the actual Mexican slang
- Everything about pronouns and adverbs

- How to talk about jobs
- Lots of grammar tips
- The main verb tenses: past, present and future
- Lots of useful phrases for shopping
- Words and phrases to go around an airport
- Cultural facts about Mexico
- The 12 most typical dishes of Mexico and how to prepare them
- How to order in a restaurant in Mexico
- What kind of music they listen to in Mexico
- The most popular songs in Mexico
- The 5 most curious and interesting Mexican festivities

... and much more!

Can you imagine how good it would feel to be able to speak Spanish like they do in Mexico? You'll be ready to have fluid conversations with other Spanish speakers! Also, no doubt, this book will be a great ally for you if you're thinking of traveling to Mexico City, Cancun, or any other Mexican destination.

So it doesn't matter if you have some notions of Spanish or if your knowledge doesn't go beyond *fiesta* and *amigo*—this book will help you anyway! From grammar to slang, from cultural facts to hundreds of useful phrases: this book is what you need if you're looking to learn to speak Mexican Spanish.

If you're ready to learn to speak Mexican Spanish in 30 days, then scroll up and click the "add to the cart" button right now!

Made in the USA
Las Vegas, NV
21 August 2023

76410897R00118